_...thought you
might enjoy
reading this
if you can keep
your head out
of the snow
long enough!!
Happy skiing_

Mayo

Ski Touring in New England

Ski Touring in New England

BY
LANCE TAPLEY

PHOTOGRAPHS BY
ANDRAS SZELENYI

Introduction by Rudolph Mattesich,
President, Ski Touring Council

STONE WALL PRESS   LEXINGTON   MASSACHUSETTS

FOR PEGGY AND ISAAC

ACKNOWLEDGEMENTS

The author would like to extend special thanks to Andy Szelenyi, Rudi
Mattesich, Bob Gray, Bob Farnsworth, Jere and Elena Daniell, Warren
Daniell, Lloyd Libby, Bob Cummings, John Waters, Dr. and Mrs. Ernest
Szelenyi, Henry Wheelwright, Burnett Buckborough, C. C. Church, Mar-
garet Morton and, above all, to Peggy.

Passages in the "Long Trail for Skiers" section of the chapter Vermont
originally appeared in, and are reprinted with the permission of, SKIING
Magazine, copyright © 1970 by Ziff-Davis Publishing Co., all rights
reserved.

A quotation in the first paragraph of the chapter Touring & the Ecology
is from John Henry Auran's column, The Sharp Edge, December, 1971,
reprinted with the permission of SKIING Magazine, copyright © 1971 by
Ziff-Davis Publishing Co., all rights reserved.

Passages in the chapters Touring & the Ecology and It's Beautiful &
It's Morally Straight originally appeared in, and are reprinted with the
permission of, the Sierra Club Bulletin, copyright © 1971 by the Sierra
Club.

A quotation in the first paragraph of the chapter It's Beautiful & It's
Morally Straight is from *The Bell Jar* by Sylvia Plath, Harper & Row,
Publishers. Reprinted with permission.

The Swix wax chart in the chapter Waxing is reprinted with the permission of the Garcia Ski & Tennis Corporation.

Copyright © 1973 by Lance Tapley

First printing
ISBN 0-913276-12X (cloth)
ISBN 0-913276-13-8 (paper)

Author's Preface

WELL, you've bought the right book, folks.

This book is considerably different from other ski touring books. While an introduction to cross-country skiing, it is also a guide to where to tour in New England.

It contains a different sort of guide, too. Descriptions of the atmosphere of a place and of personal experiences are featured alongside the more typical information of guides. This Where to Go section is the book's core, and it can be used separately from the rest.

Throughout, I have tried to write in what I think the spirit of touring should be—fun. Additionally, the New England bias of the book should be apparent in each chapter.

The book sets down the basics of equipment, clothing, technique and waxing, gives you places to go, tries to make you see the environmental significance of what you're doing, and introduces you to racing, winter mountaineering and other special activities.

Besides reading about touring, you can learn a great deal from somebody who knows how to tour, not necessarily someone who's an expert. So seek somebody out, or better, a group of people hooked on this sweet sport.

It really is sweet and it really is *simple,* and don't let anybody tell you different—not, by inference from their tone, authors of books on touring who tend to be too oriented to the disciplines of racing or mountaineering. Or who swamp the reader with over-analysis of every detail.

First and foremost, have fun.

L.T.

South Bristol, Maine

Contents

Part IV: Special Things

Appendix

Introduction

RUDOLPH MATTESICH
PRESIDENT, SKI TOURING COUNCIL

SKI TOURING has been growing steadily since its revival by the Ski Touring Council in 1962–63. It is the fastest growing ski sport in the United States and Europe. On any sunny winter day, you can now find ski tourers everywhere: on hiking, equestrian and logging trails; on abandoned railway tracks, golf courses and in their own back yards; bushwhacking, picnicking in the woods and in city parks, climbing mountains. Athletes, nonathletes, nature lovers, families which have now found a way to ski together, professional people, businessmen, teachers, people of all age groups and many occupations are following the trails in increasing numbers.

There is no way to tell just how many ski tourers there are because ski touring is a winter recreation pursued by individuals and independent groups. The only exact figures are those for the import of touring skis (mostly from Scandinavia, lately also from Bavaria), and, beginning only in 1973, figures for domestic production. These statistics show more than a 100 per cent increase from year to year. In 1972 300,000 pairs of touring skis were imported to the United States.

The sport has achieved its present status because it meets a need for an easy-to-learn, inexpensive winter recreation. Lance Tapley describes accurately how easy it is to acquire enough skill—no stress, no strain—to enjoy this sport whatever the capabilities and intent of the individual tourer. When the climbing gets too tiring, the ski tourer can settle down for a pleasant stopover, enjoy the landscape, watch the wildlife, have a little snack and a welcome drink.

Ski touring is inexpensive because it can be done anywhere

Rudi Mattesich

there is snow, because the tourer can, for an astonishingly small sum, select equipment perfectly suited to his chosen topography and intentions: wax or non-wax skis, long or short (very short for bush-whacking), wide or narrow, with or without steel edges, with toe or cable bindings; he can buy high boots or low boots; clothing is no great problem and involves no large expense . . . but there are some indications that this desirable situation might not continue.

Now, as it enters its second decade of real development, ski touring could go the way of downhill Alpine skiing, which, although it may remain the leading ski sport, seems to be reaching the limits of its growth because of rising costs and crowding brought about by overcommercialization. It is, furthermore, on a collision course with the ecologists.

Ski touring would be spoiled, also, if too much emphasis is placed on the merchandising of fancy equipment, changing fashions, on organized area skiing, and on the promotion of name resorts. The fullest advantage must be taken of the almost limitless opportunities offered by the American landscape, especially abundant in New England.

Lance Tapley's book, with its interesting and pithy text and the splendid photography by his companion Andy Szelenyi, will be a very great help in keeping ski touring what it was always meant to be—a sport which permits anyone to enjoy a pleasant outdoor recreation in the beautiful winter countryside, setting his or her own rate of speed, wearing practical, inexpensive clothing and using equipment most people can afford.

New England can truly be called a paradise for ski tourers of every degree of skill, with gentle, rolling terrain and steep mountains which attract ski mountaineers. It has many good ski touring areas and thousands of miles of trails through lovely forests.

This book will be most helpful in deciding where to go. The beginner will probably be wisest to go to a ski touring area where touring is taught, workshops are held, and conducted tours are organized. After "graduation," the tourer, well informed on safety measures, can choose from among a very great number of trails. The wonderful, healthful world of outdoor New England, with its four or five months of winter, its scenic beauty, pretty villages, and welcoming inns, is all placed before the tourer by Lance.

Happy ski touring!

Troy, Vt., 1973

Ski Touring in New England

Alpine Skiing or Cross-Country?

SOMEWHERE ALONG the lift line, Alpine skiing in New England failed.

I can best illustrate its failure by referring to a story told by a close friend, a girl with whom I grew up in Maine and who now lives near Rutland, Vt. She began skiing in the best New England tradition: scrambling around the hills and fields of our little town, practicing her christies on the rope tow slope, perfecting her parallel on weekends at Sugarloaf, which at that time was a homey, hearty ski area.

I was visiting her and her husband in midwinter. I asked her if she still went Alpine skiing.

"Not any more," she said. "Oh, occasionally we go to one of the little, out-of-the-way places around here, but we can't afford Killington."

This struck me, because they seemed to be living a fairly comfortable life, but what struck me more was her next statement:

"Anyway, I wouldn't go there even if we could afford it. It's really changed. I just don't like the people. Why, the last time I was there I asked someone for directions and he wouldn't even answer me. He just looked through me as if I weren't there. It's like being in the city."

This is why Alpine skiing failed. It *is* just like the city. Ski areas are now enclaves of many urban qualities: crowds, pollution, high prices, esthetic insult, regimentation, snobbery, callousness and crime. They're not even enclaves; the big-time ski area blight has sprawled in wide swathes through Vermont and New Hampshire.

What a shame! Originally skiing—lift skiing—was an escape from the city. Now it disappoints the city folks and discourages the country people. But the lemming instinct is powerful, and the crowds keep thronging to the downhill resorts—4 million strong nationally, it is estimated. There are signs, however, that the growth of Alpine skiing is coming to an end.

The failure of Alpine skiing came about simply because of the desire to make a fast buck. The classic American spoiler: commercialism. In the name of freedom we permitted unscrupulous profiteers to run rampant over us. We forsook planning and let "development" take its traditionally ugly course. And it was done in the American way: with advertising preying upon us, manipulating us, creating stupid desires for more and more plastic in our boots, more and more oddities to our technique, more and more status in our clothes.

Whatever happened to the desire for exercise, relief from urban numbers and pressure, the clean crisp run through the spruce? They speak to our best interests. They're not so profitable. Unfortunately, profitability for a few has been elevated over usefulness for many. The use, purpose, the *value* of skiing has sunk out of sight in a swamp of greed. It's no wonder many downhill skiers often come away with the feeling—although they try like hell to feel they had a good time—that they've been cheated.

Why is ski touring a more wholesome sport than downhill skiing?

It's cheaper.

It's easier.

It's better for your body.

It's for everybody.

It can be done almost anywhere there's snow.

It's not dangerous.

It doesn't involve crowded slopes, long lift lines, snobbery and what we mean by "plastic" things.

It preserves the environment.

It's beautiful.

Except for these last two points, which will be given separate chapters, let's take up each of my claims one-by-one.

IT'S CHEAPER

Outfitted yourself in Alpine gear lately, or better yet, outfitted your family? I mean the teenagers have just got to have those jazzy K-2 skis, right? Although *you* can get by with only $165 Heads. And those Lange super-plastic boots, at $175 a pair, are absolutely necessary to do the latest technique. You've got to have $15 gloves, $75 goose-down parkas and $65 stretch pants, of course. Equipment can cost a small family in the *thousands* of dollars. If you try to buy cut-rate stuff, the skiing magazines make you feel guilty because they say it's just not *safe,* and it certainly makes the whole family look like a bunch of hicks.

But this is only what Alpine skiing costs you *before* you get to the slopes. Let's see, weekend lift tickets for a family of four, mom and dad and two teenagers, come to about $80. Then there are those $1 hamburgers, $7 meals, and $20 motel rooms. This isn't even counting travelling costs.

Touring is something else, however. It is still possible to outfit yourself—skis, boots, poles, bindings and wax—for as little as $60 with excellent equipment, and if you splurge and spend $90 you can get some of the best made. Prices are inching up in touring, but principally what is happening is that more expensive fiberglass and plastic items are being put on the market. You don't need these. Actually most people agree that they don't work as well as traditional equipment.

And, if you wish, you can shave down some discarded Alpine skis, transform their old cable bindings so the heel can lift, and use your hiking boots and an old pair of downhill poles. Thus, cross-country skiing can cost you *nothing.* You won't be as graceful as the specially-equipped skier, and you won't get around as easily, but if poking through the fields and woods at a very leisurely pace is your thing, then by all means don't spend a cent.

You don't have to buy fancy clothing—although you can. Any old winter clothes will generally do. Even the fancy clothing doesn't cost much: $15 for knickers, $20 for a touring jacket.

There are no lift tickets to buy. At some touring "centers"—usually at downhill skiing areas—there are 75-cent to a dollar "trail fees," but these places are the exception, and you usually get a trail map for this. Of course, you don't have to ski at a touring center; just find a good woods road.

If you live in the snow belt or near it, you don't have a long drive or an expensive overnight, and it's a touring tradition—as it used to be in Alpine skiing—to pack your own meals to eat on the trail.

IT'S EASIER

There is no elaborate technique in touring, even for racers. Anybody who reads the skiing magazines discovers that current Alpine technique, now completely dependent upon owning expensive equipment, is about as simple as integral calculus. Also, many people who go downhill skiing spend a large part of their time worrying about how they look and envying the few hot-shots who can do the things everybody has been told he should be doing. And those hot-shots in turn are worrying about how they look.

Touring is, above all, relaxed. Although knowing something about form is important to fully enjoy the sport, many can get by on common sense and just shuffle around. Touring is an extension of walking, and everybody beyond a very wee age can walk.

Touring is also easy because it's what you make it: You can choose your terrain to suit your abilities and tastes. If you want to ski a short way over the flat, fine. You're not transported thousands of feet to the top of a mountain and told to get down—somehow. Which is what happens to a lot of downhill novices long before it should.

I was once at a touring center when a family—obviously fresh from the nearby Alpine area—came in to inquire about touring lessons for their little girl, who looked to be about nine years old. The father asked when tomorrow's lessons would be given.

"Well, tomorrow we have one at 1:30 in the afternoon," the manager said.

"You mean you don't have anything in the morning?" the father asked. "We'd like to drop her off here at nine."

"Why don't you do that," the manager said. "We'll just put her on some skis and she can have fun fooling around for a few hours."

"Oh, no," said the man, with a serious look, "I don't want her to pick up any wrong habits in technique. I want her to do everything right from the beginning."

Kind of a joyless attitude, if you ask me, towards skiing. The *act* of skiing should be more important than the *way* you do it. But it's typical of downhill brainwashing.

I would say that most people need only one or two lessons in touring technique. These don't have to be given by paid instructors, although they'll probably be better lessons if they are. And that statement is a consensus of touring instructors. Only racers need more technique.

It's Better for Your Body

Scientists have discovered that cross-country ski racers consume more oxygen than any other athletes. That's a pretty good indication of what touring can do for your wind. Touring, like jogging, running, bicycling and swimming, is a cardiovascular strengthener. It increases the capacity of your lungs, makes your heart stronger, the oxygen-carrying capability of the blood is increased, and you burn more fats instead of letting them deposit in your blood vessels. Your weight will be burned off, too.

If you have any interest in avoiding heart disease, the number one killer in this country, then you ought to turn to some kind of aerobic (oxygen-demanding) sport. You need this kind of activity to help prevent coronaries and to increase your ability to recover from them.

Ski touring strengthens other muscles besides the heart—nearly *all* the muscles, like swimming. Unlike downhill skiing this includes the arm muscles, which you use to pole yourself along. Cross-country skiing builds up your muscles more gradually than downhill. There aren't the violent tugs and twists which downhill submits them to, particularly when you fall at high speed down a steep slope.

There is another way touring is better for your body: It is so much more *comfortable*. The clothes aren't tight, the boots don't hurt. There are no cold, muscle-contracting rides up the chair lift.

IT'S FOR EVERYBODY

Let's face it, downhill skiing is not for everyone, despite what ski area and ski shop owners, equipment manufacturers, and hotel owners would have you believe and succeed in making you believe by spending many thousands of dollars annually for high-powered advertising.

To be a good downhill skier you must be an athlete. Even then, you have to spend a considerable amount of time skiing in order to be proficient. There's a profound joy in being able to snake down a steep slope. It's beautiful, like ballet, but most skiers never come close to doing this.

Most people go skiing only a few weekends a year. All the thrills they imagine they get out of crashing down a mountain, they could truly find in cross-country skiing, with far less danger and soreness. And if they were touring they would find it easier to ski more often.

Ski touring doesn't preclude skiing downhill. You just have a choice. Once while touring I had a six-mile downhill run. If you choose to do it, going hell-bent down a steep, narrow, curved logging road can match Stowe's National Trail for excitement.

Going as far and fast as you want over terrain of your own choice makes it possible for people of all ages and physical abilities to ski tour. I would recommend downhill skiing to only the most active middle-ager. But since touring is essentially walking on skis —until you come to a downhill run—anybody can do it. I know many older people who tour, including one group of men in their seventies who race. A child can tour as soon as he walks. Parents can take infants on a tour by strapping them on their backs.

It Can Be Done Almost Anywhere There's Snow

People in the cities can find parks to tour in; people in the suburbs can make a practice track right in their own backyard. In New England there is an abundance of woods roads, bridle trails, walks, unplowed dirt roads, fields, power lines, wood lots, reservoirs, reservations, you-name-it near almost anyone. Many people consider mountain touring the best, but that can be saved for weekends and special trips.

You also don't need packed slopes or a deep base—a few inches will be enough for many places.

It's Not Dangerous

There aren't the injuries which downhill skiing has become so famous for. Any big ski area will have at least one or two broken bones on a weekend day. I've lost count of the number of times, while skiing downhill, I've helped administer first aid to skiers who just happened to be lying there in my path, going into shock with a broken leg or ankle or arm or maybe a bad gash.

As I write this, I am looking at a newspaper clipping in which a doctor at Mary Hitchcock Memorial Hospital in Hanover, N.H., the large medical center for a major ski region in New England, says that he is astonished at the increasing number of head injuries suffered by skiers—including quite a few fatalities (two young men died on the same day, February 22, 1973, at his hospital). He concludes that the increase is partly due to equipment which lets the average downhill skier go much too fast for his own safety. He says that he has decided to equip his family with crash helmets.

No surprise to me. Several years ago at Sunday River in Maine, one of the few Alpine ski areas where I still enjoy the ambiance, two people were killed on the same day on the same trail in separate accidents. Head injuries. It was a bit icy that day. They were both good skiers.

The most disastrous touring injury I've had was a sprained ankle. And that was on a 200-mile, 14-day jaunt the length of Vermont which involved a lot of bushwacking—not your typical ski tour. I have never known anybody who broke a bone while touring. The binding (which permits the heel to be raised so a stride is possible), the skis, and all the details of the sport work to make it extremely safe.

NO CROWDED SLOPES, LONG LIFT LINES, SNOBS OR PLASTIQUE

Yes, we have no bumper-to-bumper ride up the access road, no difficulty finding a parking place, no jostling through the dense, flashy crowd, no loud and smelly restaurants, no 30-minute walks through the lift line maze (feel like a rat in a cage?), no over-confident hotdogs or paralyzed novices to crash into you with sharp steel edges, no fake-Tyrolean decor, no big-city indifference, nobody to hate because they're so damned ostentatious.

There is quietness in touring—modesty, moderation, graceful-ness—and you have a choice of solitude or real cameraderie. Join the touring counter-culture.

Definitions

Touring is recreational cross-country skiing. "Cross-country" has a racing connotation, but nowadays it is used almost interchangeably with touring. "Nordic" means Scandinavian and therefore the Scandinavian specialities in skiing: touring (or cross-country) and ski jumping. Nordic competition is cross-country racing, and jumping —as opposed to Alpine competition, which comprises downhill (nearly straight runs), slalom (runs through tight "gates" between bannered poles) and giant slalom (somewhere between downhill and slalom).

Ski tourers refer to Alpine recreational skiing (using lifts to take you up to where you can go down prepared trails or slopes) as "downhill." Alpine skiing is called that because the style originated on the steep slopes of the Alps in the early part of this century—before lifts came along, surprisingly.

There is Alpine "touring," too, just to add to the confusion. It consists of high-mountain skiing with Alpine gear modified to permit the heel to be lifted. This is also "ski mountaineering," although much mountaineering is done with Nordic equipment, quite a lot of it with light touring skis, particularly outside the West. In the West the sharp slopes above timberline and hazardous snow conditions are inimical to light skis without steel edges. There are special mountaineering skis which are nearly as light as touring skis and quite a lot lighter than Alpine skis. They usually have steel edges.

Mountaineers sometimes use "climbers," usually strips of sealskin or mohair, to enable them to tackle especially precipitous slopes. These give plenty of grip on the snow (imagine each one of those little hairs sticking in) but provide little glide (the hairs bend down the other way when the skier starts downhill; they flatten out, but not enough). "Skins" used to be quite common among the few tourers in this country 20 years ago when touring and ski mountaineering were practically synonymous, but they are rarely seen now, wax having superceded them for the most part. The new non-wax skis work on the same principal, however. Generally mountaineers now put on their crampons and take up their ice axes when their waxed skis are no longer useful.

History

FOR THOUSANDS of years the only kind of skiing was cross-country. But it wasn't touring. It wasn't for recreation, although it is not too far-fetched to imagine that Stone Age man got a thrill from a good schuss. Mainly, however, skiing was for hunting and, later, war. The oldest pictorial representation of skiing is a rock carving in northern Norway. It portrays two men on skis hunting elk (bending their knees, then, too). It is estimated the carving was made around 2000 B.C. The earliest known ski, from a bog in Hoting, Sweden, dates from 2500 B.C.

Nomadic hunters had wandered into the north as the great glaciers of the last Ice Age melted and receded. Some feel that skis probably originated where people who moved into Scandinavia originated, Asia. Significantly, early Chinese historians refer to men who have wooden horses on their feet. The first written reference to skiers, however, is in the works of the Byzantine historian Procopius, who in the sixth century mentions "gliding" Finns.

The earliest skis were made of bone, then wood, often with attached seal or reindeer skins. Some were of unequal length, the left longer, the right ski usually fur-covered for pushing off. Often one big pole was used by the skier to push himself along, a practice which did not go out of style until this century.

Skis figure in Norse mythology. Skadi, the wife of Njord, was a hunter. She roamed the mountains on "snowshoes" and could not abide living in the lowlands with her husband. Snowshoes in many ancient references meant skis, even until the nineteenth century, and so Skadi has become the goddess of skiing.

In the Middle Ages skis were used increasingly for warfare, and warriors in the northern countries were admired for their skiing prowess. In 1206 in Norway two *birkebeiner* ("birch legs" because they wore birch puttees), members of the king's guards, took the two-year-old son of the king out of danger from a group of rebels by skiing across the Dovre mountains with the child hidden behind a sword. The child, Hakon, was to become one of Norway's greatest kings. The 40-mile Birkebeiner cross-country race was instituted in 1932 to commemorate the event.

In Sweden, another annual race celebrates the journey of Gustav Vasa, the founder of the present Swedish kingdom. In 1521 he tried to arouse the inhabitants of Dalarna to throw off the yoke of the Danish King. His efforts meeting with no success, he decided to leave Sweden, starting for the Norwegian border from the town of Mora. Meantime, the Dalarnans had a change of faith and sent their best skiers after him. They met in the frontier town of Salen, 53 miles from Mora, and Vasa skied with them back to lead the rebellion. The ultimate in marathon skiing, the Vasaloppet was first held in 1922. In recent years upwards of 10,000 skiers have competed in this event, and they all start at the same time. The 90-kilometer course retraces Vasa's route, but from Salen to Mora for practical reasons.

In the 1700s Scandinavian military skiing competitions were numerous: They included jumping from roofs, slaloming between bushes and firing rifles while skiing at full speed. On the battlefields ski troops consistently wiped out troops without skis. In the same era the peasants of Norway had their own contests, such as trying to ski down a steep slope while holding a glass of beer.

In the early nineteenth century Scandinavian skiing suffered an unaccountable decline. The Norwegian Ski Division was disbanded in 1826, not to be revived until 1896. Nevertheless, some competitive skiing continued, most notably in Norway's Morgedal valley in the Telemark region. Here Sondre Norheim invented modern ski-jumping—that is, landing on a steep slope instead of the flat. In 1860 he jumped 30.5 meters, a record that held until 1893. Norheim also first tried out the Osier strap, which securely bound the toes to the skis (bindings weren't too secure previously), and he used what became known as the Telemark turn.

The first recorded cross-country race was held in Norway in 1843, but ski jumping, because of its obvious sensational appeal, was to get much of the attention devoted to skiing for decades to come. People in Scandinavia continued to ski cross-country to hunt, to visit neighbors, to go on picnics in the mountains—as they had for centuries and continue to do today. And as they do today, they profited from the techniques and equipment developed by competitors.

Norheim and the Telemark skiers ignited a revival of interest in skiing in Norway. They took Christiana (Oslo) by storm, winning all the jumping competitions, which became numerous in the 1880s and '90s. The first Holmenkollen meet, now the Nordic skiing equivalent to the World Series, was held there. Skiers at this time were generally still using one stout pole in their hands (some Lapps still do), or in the case of the boys from Telemark, only a light fir branch. Two poles were increasingly in favor in Norway, however. Skis of unequal length had fallen into disuse decades before and skins were now reserved for the mountains. Skis were often made of fragile birch, a wood native to Scandinavia, but around the turn of the century hickory, the best wood for skis, was imported from the United States by the Norwegians, as it still is today.

Worldwide interest in skiing, and particularly in setting out on trips through the mountains, was due directly to the publication and translation (into English in 1891) of *The First Crossing of Greenland* by the Norwegian explorer Fridthjof Nansen, who used skis of heavy oak. The German translation sent adventurous folk from middle European countries out on the difficult Alpine slopes, and many first ascents and glacial traverses were recorded.

The English translation inspired the wealthy few who could travel to the Alps. This area in the '90s became a fashionable winter resort, largely due to the efforts of a travel agent, Sir Henry Lunn. His son, the writer Sir Arnold Lunn, was to become the propagandist of Alpine skiing and a chief architect of Alpine competition.

The British imported Norwegian instructors to the Alps, principally to Switzerland, but more and more Alpine natives were embracing skiing, especially in Austria, where some peasants had been skiing for centuries. Here Army officers such as Major Zdarsky, Colonel Bilgeri and Hannes Schneider started adapting Norwegian styles and equipment to Alpine conditions. For one thing, a heel binding was needed for control on steep slopes.

In the mid-1920s Alpine skiing really took off. Schneider perfected the Arlberg technique, with its emphasis on the Christiana turn, and the British were winning international competitions in modern slalom, which they had invented. A great split developed in the competitive skiing world between the Norwegians and the Alpinists, with the Norwegians, because of their immense prestige, prevailing for a time. It was not until the '32 Olympics that slalom and downhill became events alongside cross-country and jumping, which were the only ski events in the first Winter Olympics at Chamonix in 1924. Alpine ski touring, however, similar to the mountain touring going on in Norway, was popular, as anyone who has read Hemingway knows.

During the first two decades of the century, there was a burst of popular interest in skiing (250,000 pairs of skis were manufactured in the U.S. in 1923, and they were for all intents and purposes touring skis), as well as a great confusion over methods. With or without poles was a question. Some people advocated going down steep slopes with eyes closed.

Fritz Huitfeldt of Telemark had invented a toe iron back in the '90s. Alpinists worked away on the heel, with the Kandahar cable binding superceding all others for touring and downhill skiing in the mid-1930s. This binding permitted up-and-down heel movement until the cable was put under hitches on the sides of the ski. The binding and modifications of it are still popular all over the world.

Meanwhile in the Nordic countries cross-country racing was beginning to rival jumping as a sport. Norway's Lauritz Bergendahl became a hero by winning the Holmenkollen 50-kilometer race consistently from 1910 to 1915. A photograph shows him using the same double-poling technique used today. "King" Bergendahl invented the modern toe or "pin" binding with pegs which fit into holes drilled into the boot's sole. In 1928 the Rottefella binding was introduced, and it changed very little over the years as it became the classic pin binding. Pins were only racing bindings for a long time; many people today in Scandinavia still prefer heel-cable bindings for touring. The modern touring and racing boots evolved from the heavier but flexible jumping boot, which, incidentally, makes an acceptable touring boot. Everyone knows which way Alpine boots went.

And everyone knows which way Alpine skiing went when ski lifts were developed in the '30s. Previously, the differences between cross-country and Alpine skiing were small except in competition. The invention of the ski lift carried Alpine to the summit of people's attention. It was easier for most people to ski, it appeared, once the climb had been eliminated and once the slopes were packed; and Alpine equipment changed to become concerned with one thing: how to go downhill faster.

But some kept the faith. It is interesting to note that Sir Arnold Lunn, in some ways the creator of Alpine skiing, was in the 1950s quite alarmed with the decadence he was seeing: the abandonment of mountaineering and touring, the reliance on lifts and packed slopes, leg-breaking speed perceived as the goal of skiers. He asked: Where was the self-reliance of the skier who could tackle all kinds of snow? Where was the close contact with nature that skiing had always facilitated? In vain. Yo-yo skiing had arrived.

SKIING IN AMERICA

I have a feeling that historians will one day find that skis just naturally spring up, a kind of spontaneous generation, whenever there's enough snow. I'm sure that the famous second use of barrel staves was not lost on enterprising colonials. But apparently the immigration of Scandinavians to this country in the 1800s (including three million Norwegians) first offered real competition to snowshoes, which is what the Indians had used.

Our most celebrated nineteenth-century Scandinavian skier was John "Snowshoe" Thompson, who carried the mail over the Sierra Nevada from California to the mining camps in Nevada beginning in 1856 and continuing for 20 years. He did 90 miles in three days. Thompson, like Nansen, used oak skis—10 feet long and weighing 25 pounds, with toe straps and a single pole. On his back were 60 to 90 pounds of mail. Thompson was born in, of course, the Telemark region of Norway and came to this country with his family as a child. On his Sierran treks he slept in caves and abandoned cabins, never carrying a blanket.

California saw many early ski exploits. Miners in Plumas County organized ski races in the 1870s, and in 1873 a record speed of 87.875 miles per hour was set over a 1804-foot course, a record which nobody today believes (that's 14 seconds).

In the 1880s ski clubs were organized in the Midwest, and jumping competitions, following Norway's lead, were then the rage. The Midwestern clubs in 1904 formed the National Ski Association and its first meets were held the following year.

The first important American international skiing competitor was Oliver Perry-Smith, who in 1909 won the first German championship, both cross-country and jumping. Perry-Smith was something of a phenomenon: In 1914 he won both the jumping and cross-country contests in the German-Austrian championships at Kitzbuhel. In many of his races he beat some of the best Norwegians.

SKIING IN NEW ENGLAND

Although the Nansen Ski Club had been organized in Berlin, N.H., well before the turn of the century, New England skiing of note

C. Allison "Al" Merrill, Dartmouth's director of outdoor affairs and former ski coach, has presided over the Nordic spirit at the college for 20 years. He is a former Olympic Nordic coach.

began with Fred Harris, a Dartmouth undergraduate who, when he matriculated, was reputed to have had the only skis on the Hanover, N.H., campus. Not for long. During the winters of 1909 and 1910 Harris organized the Dartmouth Outing Club, the most famous organization of its kind in the country, and Dartmouth men began exploring the winter outdoors which for decades they had pretty much shunned. In 1911 the first winter carnival was held, the prototype of the many now enlivening the winter college scene. In 1913 the first intercollegiate meet in the U.S. took place: Dartmouth versus McGill University of Montreal.

In those days skiing was all jumping and cross-country—and "dashes." Dartmouth graduates spread out across New England and the East, carrying the gospel of skiing to the infidels. Many alumni became teachers and coaches in public and prep schools. The foremost to propagate the word was Fred Harris himself, who went back to Brattleboro, Vt., and founded the Brattleboro Outing Club and the United States Eastern Amateur Ski Association. Brattleboro emerged as a producer of ski jumping champions. The first big jump was constructed there in 1922; the national cross-country and jumping championships were held there two years later. Since the 1920s, the Brattleboro area has been the center of Nordic competition in the U.S.

Unlike jumping and racing, touring captured few headlines, but this is what common folk began doing in backyards and on woods roads all over the country.

By 1925 slalom was included in the Dartmouth carnival, and a succession of European ski coaches changed the orientation of the country's foremost skiing college. Add to this the introduction of slalom and downhill in the Lake Placid 1932 Olympics, which started a ski fever in this country; the construction of America's first ski tow at Woodstock, Vt., in 1934; the triumphal American tours of the great Hannes Schneider—add all of this together and you have the conquest of America by Alpine skiing. Rope tows snaked up every available hill. The ski trains from Boston and New York unloaded thousands on the villages of Vermont and New Hampshire. Winter carnival in the little town of Chester, Vt., saw 4000–5000 people in attendance in 1937.

Enter World War II and the 10th Mountain Division, which brought many of America's skiers together against the Germans in Italy. When the 10th Mountain men returned after the war, many of them pursued mountain touring as a hobby in the teeth of the great Alpine boom. It was these men and a few others, mainly in New England and the Adirondacks, who were the base from which touring leaped off in the sixties.

THE TOURING BOOM

The great leap forward had several causes. In the background, of course, was the increasing frustration with Alpine skiing and the desire for an easier winter sport which was less crowded and costly. The arrival of lightweight, flexible, laminated touring

skiis—developed by cross-country competitors—was very important. Also important was the growing national awareness of the
need for exercise which began in the Kennedy Administration.
As bicycling, jogging and hiking became popular, the people who
practiced these sports needed a winter activity. As Americans became increasingly concerned with the environment, many of them
sought out wilderness experiences. Yet, it cannot be denied that
touring in the past couple of years has attracted some people because it's a fad, especially those who go to carefully-groomed
trails at touring centers. Touring fashions have even shown up in
Vogue.

But touring's growth statistics indicate that if it's a fad, it may
be with us for a while. Any curve on any graph you see goes
up, up, up. Imports of Nordic skis have been nearly doubling each
year for the past ten years. In 1968 just under 20,000 skis ar-

Putney, Vt., cross-country ski capital of the United States.

rived on our shores, but now the million mark is only a few years away.

Most of the people now touring are in the East. Indeed, New England and New York State may be said to be the hub of cross-country skiing in America. The touring boom began here in towns like Putney and Brattleboro, Vt. In some ways it may be said to have begun—to speak now of specific rather than general causes—with the publication of John Caldwell's *The Cross-Country Ski Book,* in 1964. Caldwell, the former U.S. cross-country ski coach, is coach at the Putney School. This prep school is the foremost producer of Nordic skiers in the U.S. Another focus of the revival was the annual Vermont Washington's Birthday Race begun in 1963 by Dr. Eric Barradale, a Brattleboro dentist.

People here and there picked up Caldwell's book, marathon runners and cycle racers decided to compete in the Washington's Birthday Race and converted their families and friends, touring caught on with college students, the Appalachian Mountain Club rediscovered it, and finally the ski magazines in 1970 ran features on touring. Perhaps, however, the biggest specific cause for touring's success was the effort of the Ski Touring Council and its president, Rudolph Mattesich.

1973 Washington's Birthday Race mass start—over 1000 skiers.

Rudolph Mattesich
& the Ski Touring Council

WHEN YOU MEET Rudi Mattesich you understand one reason why ski touring has charmed so many magazine and newspaper writers. Rudi ("my friends call me that") is the quintessence of charm, a courtly, tall Austrian, 72 years old, whose flawless manners and easy friendliness bespeak genuine interest in and concern for the feelings of others.

Although I had corresponded with him years ago, I met Rudi only last winter. It was a still, zero night when I pulled into the short driveway beside his 200-year-old restored farmhouse outside of Troy, at the very top of Vermont. Rudi came out to greet me. He was wearing a plaid shirt buttoned to the collar, baggy wool pants and a hearing aid. "Vell," he said, "I hope you had a good trip. Come in und have some tea."

In the neat, warm sitting room decorated with Rudi's paintings —spare winter watercolors which he exhibits in a number of galleries—we talked about the formation of the Ski Touring Council. His wife, the writer Virginia Creed, and daughter Emelia served tea and cookies. "Emmi," an art teacher in Conway, N.H., was home during a school vacation.

"Let's go back to September or October of 1962," he began. At that time Rudi was North American chief of the Austrian tourist bureau in New York, a job he held for four decades before retiring to Troy a few years ago.

He and a few friends who had been downhill skiing for years were becoming fed up with the sport. "It was boring," he said. "You never got to see nature."

Rudi looks back to inspect his troops.

He and his friends remembered the skiing of their youth. Rudi, once an officer in the Austrian Army, had taken to the Alps to tour as a means of getting away from it all during the hard times following the First World War. "Don't lose ever a war," he cautioned, knitting his brows. But those were easy days in the mountains, with extralong skis, one big pole, candle wax, skins, old army boots. It sounded like a Hemingway story of skiing in the Arlberg told by one of Hemingway's Austrian skiing partners.

Rudi and his skiing friends, many of whom had been prominent in promoting Alpine skiing, met and decided to encourage a return to trail skiing. (Rudi, too, had been prominent in developing Alpine skiing in this country. His main office back in the thirties had once cabled him: "Why don't you send us skiers?" There weren't that many skiers to send over, however, so Rudi proceeded to stir up interest by bringing Hannes Schneider to the U.S.)

The first Ski Touring Council tour was held at Mad River at Easter in 1963. The next winter the first council workshop was held at Stratton, farther south in Vermont. Workshops involve demonstrations of technique, equipment, waxing, and short tours.

The next year, 1964, the first Ski Touring Guide was published. It lists touring trails in the East, principally in New England and New York, and provides basic information about touring. Originally a thin pamphlet, now it's a booklet approaching 100 pages, filled with advertizing, and, at $1.75 each—5000 were sold last year—the source of the council's funds.

Another council publication originated at about this time, too—the Schedule, which lists council-sponsored tours and workshops. These now number in the hundreds, most of the events taking place in New England. Both publications have become indispensable to the enthusiastic tourer.

There was a false start to the council's promotional activities. Rudi and his friends first tried to enlist the support of ski areas and ski clubs. But especially at the ski areas their audiences weren't receptive. The owners were thinking of their profits. "They were afraid we would convert the downhill skiers," Mattesich said.

"It was decided we must go to the general public," he added, and this meant largely through newspaper editors and writers, who were very happy to cover an offbeat activity.

The workshops grew in number, the correspondence increased —currently at 100 letters a day. Rudi hires two part-time secretaries to help him with the mail. "We became the wholesalers of ski touring," Rudi said. "We interested the Boy Scouts, the AYH (American Youth Hostels), the Appalachian Mountain Club. First touring spread throughout New England, then to the Rockies, then California and now, finally, the Midwest, where the Scandinavians toured 100 years ago. Now the Midwest is booming, too."

For information on the Ski Touring Council, write to Rudolph Mattesich, West Hill Road, Troy, Vt. 05868. Phone: 802-744-2472. The Ski Touring Guide costs $1.75, the Schedule, of the season's workshops and guided trips, costs $2.25. Hiking trips for conditioning are held in the fall. Tours are graded for novices, intermediates and experts, but don't be too worried about your touring ability. Most tours are held on weekends and are free, but often the host to the tour or workshop will charge a $2 fee.

But along with the expanding sport came problems. During the past couple of years grumbling about the Ski Touring Council could be heard rising from the snow-covered hills of the East. Originating from those most interested in the commercial possibilities of touring, the complainers called "quaint" or "old-fashioned" the advice emanating from Mattesich. People who sold pin bindings, by far the biggest seller in America, didn't like to see the council promoting cable bindings for beginners. People who sold their services as instructors, most of them ex-racers, didn't like to hear Mattesich's casual attitude toward instruction.

Rudi defends himself: "The point is not to spend money. Levis are good. Hiking boots are good. Warm underwear and a warm shirt and sweater is all you need. Girls maybe want to look smart, but anybody can go skiing, and anywhere, too.

"The average skier is not necessarily an athlete," Rudi commented about the teaching of technique. "He should be taught within his own capabilities. Not to overdo it. Young athletic teachers take these people and put them through their paces. But many people do not go further than the walk.

"For beginners," he said, "they are better off with a little wider ski and cable bindings. Cable bindings, too, can be used with any kind of boot . . . cutting the expense, this is important."

The wider, heavier skis are not as tricky as light, narrow skis, which tend to break easier, too. Cable bindings provide more lateral support for the heel for more stability going downhill, although they don't give as much free heel play for the cross-country stride as do pin bindings, attached only at the toe. Cables are heavier, too.

As if to prove that he wasn't old-fashioned, Rudi brought a pair of Trak No-wax skis from the other room. "These are not bad," he said. "They are good for the lazy skier. And when the weather is warm. The mohair skis are good too, except when the mohair freezes." Rudi, however, prefers wooden, waxed skis.

We ended the evening's talk with Rudi predicting the continuation of touring's boom and commenting that he didn't want to

be interpreted as being against downhill skiing or the new touring centers. "We try to get along. We're not against anybody,"
he said. "If people want to have luxury, why not?"

The next morning, as if to illustrate this last point, Rudi took
me skiing on trails groomed by the North American Nordic ski
touring center in Jay.

When we started out it was still spitting snow—several inches
had drifted down during the night onto a couple feet of base; this
part of Vermont had escaped the poor snow winter of much of
the rest of New England.

Emmi joined us along with Mrs. Mattesich, who had the Trak
skis. The manager of the center was our guide. We hiked up to
the tops of several small hills less than a mile from the shop and
stopped at an abandoned sugarhouse. Just before we reached it, a
rabbit suddenly scampered across our path, and, chasing it, two
big dogs. But the rabbit jumped into a thicket right before our
eyes, and the dogs sped past.

It was a friendly, talkative, scenic stroll—the faint snowfall
covered the nearby hills with a veil of gauze. Rudi and wife and
daughter shuffled along. No racers they. Neither was I, but at one
point, because I hadn't worn enough clothing, I strode off at a
rapid clip down a trail to warm up. When I returned, the touring
center manager, who apparently felt that the slow pace cramped
my style, remarked, glancing at the others: "Come back some time
and I'll show you some good skiing."

I hope he had a good time that morning. I did. It was good
skiing.

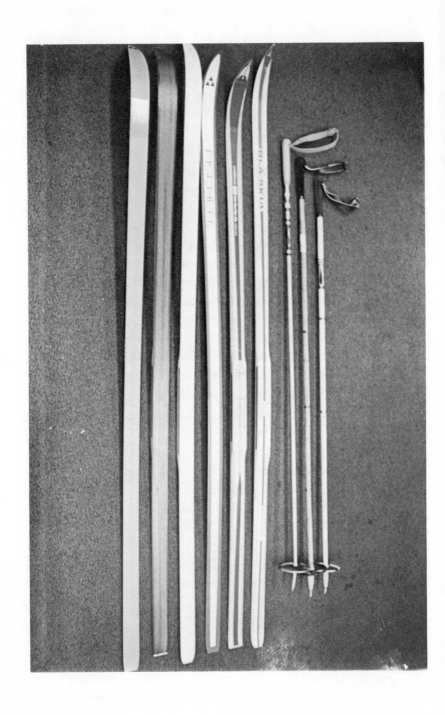

Equipment

The Short Course

GO TO a reputable dealer in cross-country gear and say: "I would like to buy some ski touring equipment, please."

The Long Course

SKIS

The general characteristics of cross-country skis are lightness, narrowness, flexibility and lack of steel edges. They are considerably more flexible, several centimeters narrower and much lighter than Alpine skis. Most are wood, the bottoms likely of hickory. Instead of the steel edges of Alpine skis there will generally be something lighter, but it will be harder than the rest of the bottom, such as lignostone—pressed beechwood.

The skis are narrow and without steel edges to cut down on the weight. They are flexible for varying terrain and because wax works better when it is always in touch with the snow. Their soft tip is also useful for slithering over the bumps. X-c skis also have camber, like Alpine skis, but more of it. The bend of each ski in the middle is camber. When you step on a ski, the bend is eliminated and your weight is then evenly distributed over the ski. Camber helps make x-c skis springy—good for striding.

There are several tests you can make to judge the quality of skis. If you put the skis together and press them so the edges touch, they should flatten smoothly and completely together. This will show you if there's any warp. This also is an indication of the general flex of the ski—whether it is stiff or soft. Softer skis for lighter people and powder addicts (are there any in New England?). Stiffer skis for heavier and ice-prone people.

Make sure the camber of one ski matches the camber of its mate. In fact, check the serial numbers to make sure you've got the mate. More camber for heavier people; less for lighter. Test the camber for you by standing on the skis; you should be able to just slide a thin sheet of paper under each ski.

The time-honored way for determining ski length is still valid —stand and raise your arm straight up. The ski tip should come to your wrist or thereabouts. The more laminations (separate pieces) and layers, the more unlikely your skis will lose their shape. Generally, the best touring skis come from Norway. Sorry about that, Sweden and Finland. You can rarely go wrong with good Norwegian brands like Bonna, Asnes, Toppen, Blaski, Split-kein, etc. Norwegian snow conditions are similar to New England's.

Price is probably the most important test you will give skis. Last year you could buy superb light touring skis for under $40. Prices are going up, though. Hickory is expensive.

RACING SKIS

These weigh about three pounds and are mostly under 48 milimeters wide. Their interior often has a lot of balsa, and their running surface will be most likely of birch or plastic. The tip bends up at a more pronounced angle because the stronger stride of a racer tends to lift the tail of the ski off the snow, bringing the tip down and back—and if it catches in the snow that could mean the race. These skis have sacrificed durability for lightness. They should never be an initial investment for a tourer. After you've skied a bit and want to try some races, they're fine as second skis. You should know, however, that casual "open" races are frequently run on light touring skis. Jarvinen of Finland is famous mainly for racing skis.

Wide difference: downhill ski, left, and light touring ski.

LIGHT TOURING SKIS

This is probably the biggest seller now. They are a good compromise between racing lightness and touring durability and are fine for both prepared track and woods road touring. Some models, like the wider and heavier Bonna 2000s (averaging four pounds, 12 ounces, 52 mm), are good all-around skis. I race my Bonna 2000s (I do poorly) and I have climbed on Katahdin with them. Light touring bottoms are usually hickory, the edges lignostone.

TOURING SKIS

Bonna's next model, the 2400, is a good example of this type. It's hickory-bottomed, lignostone-edged and is 55 mm wide and weighs a hefty five pounds or more depending on length. This is the kind of stable ski the Ski Touring Council recommends (55 mm or over). Some touring skis go over 60 mm and approach six pounds. If you plan to spend most of your time bushwacking, and you don't care about weight, this may be the ski for you. But I think light touring skis are just as good for as rugged terrain as you'll find in New England.

MOUNTAINEERING SKIS

These skis are built much like Alpine skis. And they're big. The 210 mm Asnes mountaineering ski weighs seven pounds, nine ounces, and is 65 mm wide. It has steel edges and a running surface of hickory. The Bonna model 35 is similar. I doubt if these skis are necessary in New England unless you do all your skiing in the Presidentials and on the upper reaches of Katahdin.

As far as the bottoms of touring skis are concerned, hickory is still the best bet. Birch, although it holds wax better, is too soft for our conditions. Plastic or fiberglass-treated bottoms, which racers are starting to use more, are of uncertain value. They don't require base preparation, but some kinds don't hold wax as well as hickory. For edges: lignostone, plastic, or simply an all-hickory ski—but the edges will wear down faster.

Home-made skis are discouraged in most books and, of course, commercial catalogs. But I know people who've trimmed down old hickory Alpine skis and had a fine time with them. The savings and pride in workmanship obviously had something to do with their enjoyment. Take the steel edges off and cut the skis narrower. The wooden edges will round off, though, and the ski will be heavy and not lively. They should be blocked for storage as skis of one piece or few laminations warp easily.

Perhaps the future in touring belongs to synthetic skis, as the present does already in Alpine skiing. It was inevitable that fiberglass and metal skis would appear on the market as soon as touring proved profitable. Synthetic skis are more expensive. Also, our technology has an impetus of its own, a knee-jerk reflex to answer any demand even if it is already well answered.

At present, synthetics aren't better. Wax generally doesn't stay on as well and they don't have the right flexibility. They are, however, nearly impossible to break. Fischer, the world's biggest ski manufacturer, has come out with some interesting metal skis—very light, and their flexibility seems quite good. You can't really go wrong with skis like this, especially as a beginner.

NON-WAX SKIS

This is the revolution. It's a revolution which already has succeeded—at least for a permanent good-sized chunk of the market. And if these skis are perfected, for most of the market.

Nevertheless, they don't glide very fast. However, they are *easy* to use. That whole messy business of waxing is eliminated. For me, waxing is fun. It's enjoyable to gain expertise in this area, and it's not that difficult. I even enjoy smoothing out klister (soft wax) with my hands, but apparently there are a lot of people coming into the sport now who wouldn't ski if they had to spend time waxing. Fine. I think most people, however, are still going to opt for waxable skis, and I recommend them to most people. But better non-wax skis than no skis at all.

Non-wax skis work fairly well under many snow conditions. On a day when the snow is clogging all waxes, a pair of Trak fish-scales may be the best skis around. And when you have a few minutes after work to get a quick tour in, your Skilom mohairs can be used just as quickly as you can fit your boots into their bindings.

I prefer the fish-scale type because mohairs lose effectiveness when they get soggy from wet snow or when they freeze. A new product is being developed by the 3M company called Fibre-tran which claims to be impervious to moisture. One curious characteristic of mohair skis: You have to be careful to keep them flat on the snow because if you tilt the ski to one side you may be lifting one of the mohair tracks off the surface, losing traction.

The Trak skis have the disadvantages of wearing out easily and of living up to their name in that they "track" too well. They don't have the smooth lateral sliding quality of waxed skis, which is important for easy turning. They also have the disadvantage of humming or singing as they go down a slope. I like quiet in the woods.

BINDINGS

Cable binding or pin binding? The Ski Touring Council has recommended cables for beginners because they offer more stability going downhill—less lateral heel movement is permitted. But most shops and touring centers are pushing pin bindings. This is partly because most people running these places have a racing background, but it also is due to the worldwide trend toward lighter, freer cross-country gear.

I recommend the pin binding for the beginner, but the cable binding is not bad. You often can use hiking boots with cable bindings. This is an advantage with children but some cable apparatuses are too big for kids' skis. If you have a heel plate with your pin binding, as you should, not only will it keep the snow from clogging under the heel, but, if you keep your heel pressed down on it when going downhill, the friction will give you some lateral support and, skiing downhill gets easier rapidly as you gain experience. Also, the

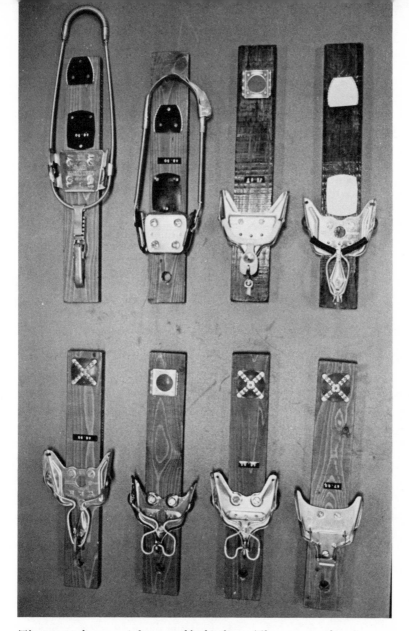

*The two at bottom right are cable bindings. The rest are the pin type.
Notice the heel plate with each binding.*

cable binding does not permit as free a stride and is heavier. Finally,
with cable bindings, especially if you get a front-throw cable binding with a hitch you can put the cable under on each side of the

How it's done: too simple for words.

ski, you may get going too fast for your nonsteel edges to control you. When you fall the bound-down heel is more dangerous than a free heel (no safety release, you see).

Pin proponents will tell you that if you get a good fit, you don't have to worry about the lateral support. It is very important to get a good fit. Most pin bindings have three pegs which fit into holes already drilled into the soles of the boots. You jam your boot into the toe iron. A bail, which pushes down on the top of the extended sole, is pressed down and latched to a little metal knotched claw in front of the toe iron. Very simple. Make sure that the toe iron isn't too big. Binding and boot sizes are standardized. The toe of the boot should fit *very* securely into the toe iron.

You wouldn't think, to look at pin bindings, that technology could possibly improve on them. It hasn't, but it's trying hard, mainly with devices (like the Kloa) that stick right through the toe of the boot, or "step-ins" with iron plates on the toe which lock into the binding. The disadvantage here is that you have to use special boots.

The most available pin bindings are Rottefella, Troll and Villom. Some have contraptions that allow you to release the boot from the binding by pressing with your ski tip point. If you're not willing to bend over, give up. Some binding bails come out too easily—they are usually held in by pressure only. This happened to a friend when we were on the Appalachian Trail in the Presidentials once, and he lost it in deep snow and didn't have a replacement. He tied his boot onto the binding with some extra bootlaces, but he spoiled the tranquility of the rest of the day by lots of moaning and groaning and scandalous language. He should have had an extra bail. I avoid this problem by buying bindings that have the bails solidly attached to the toe iron.

The people who sell you bindings will mount them for you. If you choose to do it yourself, you have only to follow directions.

Storing Equipment

This is easy. We're going to make it easy, anyway. Naturally, there are diametrically opposed schools of thought about how skis should be stored. One says block the skis, another says it's useless. One says keep moisture out of the skis, another says let 'em soak up water in a snowbank.

The Tapley Rule: Adopt the easiest of two conflicting theories. So don't do anything to your skis. Don't take off the last coat of wax. Don't block them. Simply stand them in a closet and forget about them until the fall. I could justify this advice with elaborate technical explanations, but I'm not going to. It works. It's easy.

Same with boots. Although it would be nice, as with all boots, not to let them get mildewed by keeping them in a relatively dry place.

Don't worry about poles or bindings either. For your wool clothes, keep the moths away with mothballs.

Finally, for the wax, if you can keep it in a cool place, the better. Otherwise, waxes will eventually all ooze out of tubes and tins and mix together in a real multicolored mess.

BOOTS

There's a debate here, too. Pretty much the same sides are lined up against each other: the proponents of the higher-cut, heavier touring boot (they look like hiking boots) and those who say what you need are lightweight items resembling track shoes—what x-c racers wear.

The debate has had a lot of the soul knocked out of it in the past few years by the introduction of boots midway between the extremes of these two kinds. I would suggest this compromise to most people. It is often called the "light touring boot."

The heavier boots sometimes have cable notches on the heel. But you can use them with pin bindings. The lateral support controversy pops up when it comes to boots. Stiffer, higher uppers may give more lateral support for downhill running. Someone with weak ankles should look at heavier, more secure boots.

The lower-cut boots feature lightness. I started out with higher boots. As I feel much more secure on my feet, for touring I now prefer semiracing boots because of lightness and absolute flexibility. In the winter I wear this kind of boot all the time because it is water-resistant, strong yet comfortable, and I don't have to change my footwear to go skiing.

I've skied nearly everywhere in New England with this kind of boot, but I'm not sure I would recommend it to someone who didn't have skiing experience and planned to ski off the prepared track. Maybe you could hack it if you've had Alpine experience. For most people, try one of those slightly heavier, stiffer, higher models.

The uppers should be breathable. Old-fashioned leather still is the best. It can be silicone-treated but it should not be waterproof. Resistant to water, yes, but otherwise your feet will get too sweaty.

The soles should of course be flexible so you can stride. (A far cry from the latest entry in the cement overshoe field—Alpine boots.) Don't worry about the warmth of the boots; your feet are always bending up and down. They won't get cold unless you've got very light racing boots and are not racing in them. The uppers probably should be stitched to the soles, but I've got a glued-together pair and they haven't come apart after a good winter's wear.

Be very discriminating in fit. Blisters and lost toenails take all the fun out of ski touring. Try boots on with the same kind and number of socks you'll be wearing while skiing. Remember that your feet will be pushed around in them, so try on a lot of pairs and walk around. Look for a comfortable break to the uppers. Better not to err, but if you do, err on the big side (you can always put on heavier socks).

POLES

You have your choice of traditional bamboo—Tonkin cane—or aluminum or fiberglass. The bamboo poles average $7–$8; the others are two to three times as expensive (mostly used by racers).

Don't try to get by with old downhill poles unless you're out

At extreme left, a child's touring boot. Then, from left to right, boots from heavy to light, from mountaineering to racing.

The two poles on the left have curved tips. The whole end is curved on the pole third from left. These are cross-country poles. The pole at the right is for Alpine. It has a straight point.

not to spend a cent for touring gear, which is such an admirable end that any means justifies it. The downhill poles won't have the curved tips necessary to be easily snagged in the snow and for easy extraction from it.

The straps should be adjustable. The baskets should be bigger for touring than racing—so the pole won't sink in the deeper snow tourers go through. The old stand-by for pole length still holds: They should fit just under the armpit.

The main difference between downhill and x-c poles is flexibility. Cross-country poles are springier. They help you spring along. Bamboo poles, though far less expensive, have plenty of spring, and they're surprisingly sturdy.

CARING AND REPAIRING

Skis don't need much care. If skis get severely gouged over rocks, you can shave the bottoms—if you've got wooden skis. If you've got a synthetic bottom you may be able to use one of the preparations Alpine skiers use to patch them up. Be careful when applying heat to your ski bottoms (see section on waxing). Charred skis are unsightly and don't wax too well.

Simple pin bindings have given me the biggest problem of all my equipment. Screws are always coming loose. Think of the strain on them. Once I didn't pay much attention to a loose screw and I lost a pair of skis. A crack appeared around the screw hole and eventually split the ski. Keep screws tight. When they come loose, plug them with broken matchsticks and epoxy. Out on the trail, use twigs—then twist the screw in.

Use shoe polish on your boots. And silicone if you wish to make them a little more water-resistant. Poles? If they're bamboo you can tape them if they start to crack. But once a good crack appears, a pole's life is limited. I've taped up and used poles that were completely splintered—in an emergency.

ADDITIONAL GEAR

Waxing gear, food, first aid kit, survival equipment and clothes will be taken up in separate sections.

Here's a list of what you might also like to take along, particularly for day trips.

· Spare ski tip, plastic or metal. This is a must to carry in your pack.

· Pack. There are many small packs ideal for day trippers. Fanny packs may be adequate. There are special ski tourers' rucksacks which allow the load to be carried low and close to the body—what the skier needs for stability. These are generally larger than what I use, the mountain climber's teardrop pack, which is so small I force myself not to carry too much. But I find them perfectly adequate for day trips, and they are the ultimate in stability.

· Dark glasses. Also a necessity.

· Rawhide or some strong cord which can be used for fabricating a makeshift pole strap, binding or shoelace.

A touring pack: stable, inexpensive and a handy outside pocket

· Extra binding bail, extra screws for the binding, electrical tape for repairing bamboo poles.

· Drinking cup. Sierra Club cup can be used for bowl and plate, too.

· Canteen.

· Pencil and paper.

· Combination knife. Swiss Army type. My friends always get the model with the corkscrew. The awl comes in handy, too. And the screwdriver-bottle opener.

· Sunburn lotion.

· Pack thermometer. Great for waxing and just a great all-around gadget.

Clothing

To be well prepared for the capriciousness of New England's winter climate, the well-dressed tourer should probably wear a set of yellow fishermen's foul-weather slickers, goose-down long underwear, and carry a pair of ice skates.

In short, it's bloody difficult to know how to dress for weather that can go from a bitter 10 below to a rainy 40 degrees, while you're enduring a blizzard and a sleet storm along the way—all in a matter of hours.

But there are several general principles which can be followed:

1. Because of the exercise, ski touring keeps you warm. You may not need many clothes even when the temperature is well below freezing. However, sometimes the temperature can really fall, with an accompanying rise in the wind, and you'll need more clothes. Also, when you stop moving more clothing will be needed. The answer is to take extra clothes along on a trip.

2. You want lightweight garb to make exercise easier; you want loose clothing so the body can stride freely. The answer here is clothes of certain fabrics.

3. You need clothes that are breathable because your exertion will produce perspiration; you need some kind of protection against rain and snow. Water-resistant clothing is the best compromise.

These points in mind, let's go from head to toe:

HEADGEAR: An Alpine ski cap is good. A lot of heat is lost through the head, so by keeping a hat on, you may be able to get by with less bulky clothing. Notice that cross-country racers almost always wear hats even though they may have only a turtle-neck on. Furthermore, hats keep snow from branches out of your hair and keep long hair from getting in your eyes.

TORSO: Keep this warm and the rest of you will be warm. But breathability is important here too. So, I wear a Norwegian fishnet undershirt. The air cells created when you slip a shirt or turtleneck over it insulate you and allow moisture from the skin to escape to outer layers of clothing.

The turtleneck, you may have forgotten, was designed to protect the neck, which also gives off a lot of heat. Get one that is cotton or has lots of cotton in it, and it will be breathable. For tempera-tures above 25 degrees this may be all you'll need when you're moving.

You'd better have along a windbreaker of some sort, though. I prefer poplin—it's breathable—to nylon. Don't get a waterproof one, just water-resistant.

I also like to carry in my pack, and occasionally put on, a miraculously light, warm, down vest which packs into a bag. In place of this you can pack, or tie around your waist, a sweater or heavy wool shirt.

GLOVES: For cold weather, Alpine ski gloves are good. Other-wise, you might want plain old work gloves with a pair of silk liners in your pack. Cheap gloves are nice because you don't mind getting wax on them or scraping them as you try to save yourself by grabbing a tree, etc. Touring keeps your hands warm; above freezing you won't be wearing gloves at all. There are x-c racing and touring gloves. They are very breathable (full of holes), but expensive. Mittens are warmer than gloves, but they may be too warm.

TROUSERS: Classically, ski tourers wear knickers. Only a few years ago there were few knickers on the market besides the expen-sive corduroy Alpine kind. Now there are many of a better mate-rial for x-c: poplin. There are knickers made from other porous

The well dressed skier: Jim Daley with Alpine cap, wool shirt, knickers, knicker socks, fanny pack, gloves (but not for rubbing on klister). Nice skis, too. And a beautiful day.

materials. Or you can make your own. I have a pair made from $3.98 work pants. Just sew in a little nylon belt on each cut-off leg bottom. I also have a pair of racing knickers—jazzy blue stretch pants with plastic on the inside front of the leg to break the wind. They're great if you're willing to spend the money. I must confess that these are the most comfortable knickers I've ever worn, but I wouldn't wear them bushwacking.

Knickers are preferred by tourers because they're loose for the knee-bending cross-country stride. So you see why Alpine stretch pants won't do. Any loose pants will. Wool will keep you warmer. I often tour in jeans, which aren't loose at first, but soon get flexible enough.

You don't have any long underwear? Many times you will be

plenty warm with knickers and knicker socks, which come above the knee, but at times you won't. Wool underwear is the best because it insulates when wet. There are cotton thermal knits for people who don't like the feel of wool on their skin. Old-time New Englanders prefer red longjohns.

SOCKS: If you've got knickers, knicker socks are necessary. They come in nifty Norwegian patterns and plain blue and red. The smoother the finish the less snow will stick to them. You should generally have on two pairs of socks. Either knicker socks or heavy wool socks on the outside. On the inside try thin wool white socks, the kind you can buy at sport, mountain, and, sometimes, ski shops. An extra pair of socks, which can double as extra mittens, is a must for a day-long hike.

GAITERS: Here we come to a special cross-country item which can be done without in New England, but life can be easier if you have them. They keep the snow very effectively out of the boot. That is until they get wet and freeze and then hang uselessly.

There are special cross-country stretch outfits—my blue knickers are the bottom half of one. These are expensive, but they sure are stylish. As I indicated earlier in the book, though, you don't really have to buy any new clothes for ski touring. In fact the older the clothes, often the better they are suited for touring. I've seen some wild duds on ski tourers. One friend wears a ragged old fleece-lined coat he had given to him in Afganistan. Another wears a Canadian Army field coat which trails in the snow as he glides along.

Technique

DON'T WORRY ABOUT IT

THIS chapter makes no claim that it is the definitive work on cross-country technique. It is for beginners; it is an introduction. But in a brief space it contains all most people need to know about technique—at least from a book. Skiing with someone who knows how will teach a person a lot. Professionally-given lessons might be desired, too. However, despite the present elaborate codifications and analysis of technique à la Alpine, few lessons are necessary for most people.

For those interested in racing technique, reading books might be a desirable supplement to advice from a good coach. Caldwell's, Brady's, and Lederer and Wilson's books contain detailed probings of what happens in touring motions. For the beginner a detailed analysis can be confusing and deadening. Why get so worried about what you're doing? That's the worst thing possible for your technique.

Relax. It's easy.

BASIC SHUFFLING

Even if the conditions are rotten . . . don't delay! Get out there in your backyard and put your gear on.

Next move: Do whatever you want. Get around somehow. No. I'm not going to tell you how to walk. Falling down might be a good idea at this point. To break the ice, as it were. That'll be all you'll break, because falling isn't dangerous on cross-country skis— your heel is free. The ultimate safety binding. Just sort of non-

chalantly sit down on the snow to the side, breaking your fall with
your hands. The first difficulty for beginners is the fear of falling.
Makes you all tense. Fall a few times and you'll become an expert
at it. After a half-hour (or 10 minutes, or a day, or a week) of the
do-it-yourself basic shuffle, you'll hit upon a few motions that you
would like to refine, such as . . .

TURNING AROUND

With your skis parallel six to eight inches apart (a sensible distance
for most maneuvers on the flat and going uphill), move the tip of
one ski a foot or two away from the other. Keep the tails together.
Bring the other ski tip over parallel again to the ski you've moved.
Repeat. As you can see, you can do this in a complete circle. You've
probably already hit upon it anyway.

By the way, what have you been doing with your poles? Using
them to keep your balance, right? Good idea. Make sure you're
holding them correctly: Reach up *under* and through the strap,
which should be adjusted just loosely enough so when you throw
your hand in back of you, your thumb and forefinger have the top
of the pole between them.

WALKING, STRIDING

Another basic motion you're already doing which perhaps could be
refined. This is *the* basic motion of touring. You have undoubtedly
already noticed that when you walked with your skis, the forward
ski had a tendency to glide a bit as you shifted weight onto it.
Working on that glide is the essential idea of cross-country striding.

Notice that if you flex your knees a little more you will glide
more. If you keep your skis on the snow instead of picking them
up as you walk, your glide will be enhanced. Just slide them along.

What about those poles? Feel confident enough to let them hang
for a while? Do that and try this: Pretend you are a kid with a
scooter. Push off with one foot. As you push off with that foot
extend the other foot forward. As you pump away, rhythmically

Olympic gold medalist Babben Damon, left, has perfect touring form. Jack Lufkin—a former Olympian, too—briskly strides up a hill.

shift weight to the forward foot and glide it ahead. It helps to be in a track somebody has already set, and of course you should be on a flat. Don't do any leaping. Just shift the weight and glide forward.

Now try alternating feet while pushing off and gliding. Hum a little tune. Keeps your mind in rhythm. Push. Glide. Push. Glide. Slow and easy.

Have you noticed that your shoulders, just as in walking, want to move your arms as you slide along? Let them. Swing your arms forward and back, holding your poles—keeping them still out of the snow—directed in back of you. Push. Glide. Swing along. That hiking song, "I Love to Go A-Wandering . . ." etc., is nice to sing at this time.

You will have remarked that, as in walking, your left arm comes forward as your right foot goes forward. Feel this rhythm for a while. Next, hold your pole with the tip inclined a foot or so backwards, and, as you swing your arm out, touch the tip to the snow. Gradually, you may find yourself naturally wanting to use the pole to give yourself a little push, and the push back should come just as you straighten the knee on the opposite side of the body, pushing off with that leg. Plant the pole more firmly, keeping the elbow bent. Now you are using both pole and leg to push yourself forward.

This is the basic "diagonal" style of cross-country skiing, used by racers and tourers alike. It's no big deal. The major difference between racers and tourers is that racers stride better and faster.

It is called diagonal because of the natural swing of the body which brings the left arm forward when the right leg is forward, and vice-versa. It is a perfectly natural motion. It is simply an extension of walking. If in doubt that what you're doing is right, remember: Walking is what you're doing.

If you've read anything else about technique you may be wondering where the "kick" is. The word "kick" is probably the most misused term in the cross-country skiing lexicon. I have used the word "push" instead. But what you need to concentrate on is the *glide*. And the push will take care of itself.

The important thing is to be relaxed. Don't be all hunkered over. As you ski, you'll be a little lower than when you're standing still because your body will naturally be inclined slightly forward, with your knees bent.

Have a relaxed grip on your poles. Put the weight, when you push off, on the *straps*. As you bring the pole behind you, release the hold, with the tube resting between the thumb and forefinger. With a more powerful stride you'll be pushing off so vigorously that the arm should follow through and extend almost straight back. Keep your arms close to the body. Don't swing your arms with the elbows pointing way out.

You've probably seen many pictures of x-c racers with the tail of the rear ski up in the air. These photos are misleading to many tourers. Don't pay any attention to this—it will just be extra work. Touring has to be natural. Like so many other aspects of sports, you can't just go through the motions. It's got to mean something. As you develop more powerful strides, the tail will automatically lift up. Good racers lift their ski tails a foot or more.

Some people twist their hips, swinging them around as they shift their weight, and literally leap from one foot to another. This style, thought by some to be an aggressive way to ski, is also wasted motion. You want to go straight ahead in the track. No vectors to the side.

A tip: Most beginners trying to get the x-c stride pat bob around too much. As you stride, try to remember to keep your head in a straight line.

If you can do all I've just described, you've surpassed basic shuffling and you're a good skier—at least over the flat. I've put this information together because I wanted to show how integral striding is with walking, how interrelated all of these motions are. You won't be able to smoothly accomplish all I've described on the first day. But in a few days you should be getting there. Meanwhile, start working on other aspects of technique right away. All technique is integrated.

STRIDING UPHILL

A variation of striding over the flat. Pick first an easy uphill slope. If you find yourself slipping backwards a bit, bend forward a little more. Shorten your movements. You may have to exert yourself a bit with your poles, but remember that skiing—especially uphill—is done mainly by the legs, not the arms. Zip. Up the slope. Not bad. (More on this shortly.)

DOWNHILL

With a bow to the Alpine skiers, this is really the part of skiing that is most fun. Even on those tricky narrow little touring skis.

Pick a slope that has such a gentle outrun that you'll come to a stop naturally. Push off with your poles, both at once (welcome to double poling). Keep your feet a little farther apart than you had them when striding. Let each act independently; we are bipeds. Hold your hands a bit forward at waist level. Bend from the waist slightly. Flex knees slightly. Also flex the ankles, with heels pressed on the ski. Repeat on the same gentle slope a few times. Try an occasional flexing of the knees greatly—scooching down quite a lot without bending the upper body forward and sticking out the rear. This is simply to loosen up.

Above all, don't bend way forward, sticking your bottom out behind you. This is the flag of all beginning skiers, Alpine or Nordic. With cross-country skis attached only at the toes, you'll soon find yourself pitching forward more than you planned. This is only injurious to the pride. Remember to keep the heel down. Feel the snow surface with its little irregularities right through the skis and the bottoms of your boots.

Bring the skis a little more together. Bend your knees when you go over a bump or when any change in the snow is encountered. Practice falling to the side—that sitting-down technique—as you're going along. You might even try falling forward; as long as you protect your face you'll be okay. Try different terrain, faster terrain. If you are going along the side of a hill, put most of your weight on the downhill ski and slide your uphill ski a few inches in advance. Welcome to the traverse. Practice double poling.

If you've advanced to the stage where you'll be facing some worrisome bumps, simply bend the knees as you take them. Or extend one ski a foot ahead of the other and flex the knees as you take the bumps. Welcome to the Telemark position.

KICK TURN

This maneuver changes the direction of your skis 180 degrees while standing in one spot. With the weight on your uphill ski, bracing yourself with your poles and your edges, lift the tip of your downhill ski way in the air, twist your foot and bring the ski down *facing in the opposite direction* in the same track it was in before. Your body now may seem all twisted up. The way to unwind it is simply to swing around the uphill ski parallel to the other ski, shifting your weight onto the other ski at the same time. Your poles will take

Frank Fetter of Hanover, N.H.,
terror of the over-70 racing cir-
cuit, in a snowplow. Most people
prefer to put their poles behind
them, but maybe he's going to
spring off a mogul.

care of themselves. If you're not on a steep hill, forget the "down-hill," "uphill" nomenclature.

SNOWPLOWING

The humble snowplow, so scorned in Alpine skiing, is Nordic skiing's mainstay. You can do almost anything with it.

First, you can slow down and stop. As you're sliding down a slight incline, spread the tails of your skis apart, keeping the tips together. This forms a "V" position. You do this by turning inward your knees and ankles, so that the inside edges of your skis scrape or push against the snow. Practice standing still at first, then on steeper and steeper hills. What happens is that the more you bite the snow with your edges and the farther apart your skis, the more you will slow down and the quicker you will bring yourself to a stop. Make sure you don't stick out your *derrière,* as they say in the French technique, by leaning too far forward. Your heel has to remain firmly on the ski. Lowering your *derrière* (flexing the knees), however, will allow you to apply more pressure to the edging.

Turning can also be accomplished by snowplowing. Simply bear down more on the right ski and you will turn to the left, and vice-versa. You bear down on the right ski by pushing your right knee in more than the left, making it edge more. Also lean the upper body a little out towards the right. This, too, will turn you to the left. (Your right ski, remember, is *pointed* towards the left; weighted, it becomes the controlling, steering ski.)

Modifications of this simple turn are endless, according to the demands of the terrain and the skill of the skier. One thing you can do, and probably will do more often than a precise snowplow, is the *steered turn*—putting your weight more on the right ski if you are turning to the left, edging, pressing on the heel and steering around a curve without going into a snowplow position. You may have to *stem* that ski (a half-snowplow position) to get the right effect.

Invent your own turns to suit the snow and terrain. This is what all the best skiers do. Nobody ever skis with the exact turns described in books.

When you're going with some speed down a hill and want to turn to the left, you can steer with both your *inside* (and uphill) and outside (or downhill) skis, flexing your knees, particularly the uphill one, pressing down on the heels, and leaning the hip inward against the centrifugal force while the upper body remains more upright. (Holy smokes, now you're doing angulation!) It helps if it's a woods road banked to the outside by other skiers or snowmobiles, so your downhill and outside ski will be lifted by the terrain and will get weighted automatically. I call this the *banking* turn. It is a kind of parallel turn, like the steered turn, which also requires some angulation.

ADVANCED SHUFFLING

STEP TURN

This is a very common turn in the repertoire of tourers who have been at the sport a little while—although you may be able to master it the first day, particularly if you've had any Alpine skiing experience (this goes for all the technique I've mentioned).

If you want to step turn to the right, lift the right ski tip and

Lenny Amburgey executes a snappy step turn.

point it where you want to go. Don't be too ambitious at first. As you place it down in the snow, lift the other ski and place it parallel in the new direction. Very helpful while skiing in prepared tracks where snowplowing is difficult; where, indeed, snowplowing may even damage the track.

DOUBLE POLING

A great change of pace. Faster, but more tiring. Simply push back with both poles at once. Don't start off with the arms locked parallel in front of you. Keep a crook in them—you'll get more power. Bend the upper body forward over the poles before pushing backwards. Follow through winding up with the arms in back of you stretched almost straight back. Your upper body should be still leaning forward at this point. In fact, you should have lunged it forward. Arms should come back to normal just as the upper body leans back erect. Make fluid, powerful strokes: coil, uncoil.

You can combine double poling with striding. The stride actually is done between pushes of the poles. Push one leg back, gliding forward on the other, as you bring the arms forward to pole. As you plant the poles, the leg that has done the pushing should be beginning to come forward. As you push off with the poles, the body weight firmly over them, the two legs should be nearly parallel again. What it is: Simply, pushing off with one leg between pole pushes. Alternate legs.

SIDESTEP

Get perpendicular to the fall line (the imaginary line which goes straight downhill). With the weight on the downhill ski, lift or slide the uphill ski up the hill a few inches. Set the edge into the snow. Lift the downhill ski up parallel to it. Shift weight onto downhill ski again, setting its inside edge meanwhile. Repeat. Good for climbing very steep sections.

DIAGONAL UPHILL

For steeper pitches than what we've earlier talked about, the diagonal has to be modified a little. It all depends if you've waxed well, but you should be able to scurry over most hills straight on. "Scurry" is a key word. Don't hesitate. Keep moving. Chug to yourself: "I know I can. I know I can." You might have to scootch down more, but what you almost certainly have to do is: *Go up on your toes.* Keep your forward knee over the foot, too. Prance over the hill.

TRAVERSE

You might not be able to take a hill straight on, though, so zig-zag up it, performing step turns at the end of a zig or a zag, or kick turns or simply scurry around to the opposite direction. You can combine the traverse with side-stepping. You also can do downhill traversing. Remember that the traverse position while coasting demands weight on downhill ski, advance the upper ski slightly.

HERRINGBONE

The basic form is a snowplow in reverse. Really in reverse: You do it going uphill. Plant your skis, tips apart, in a "V," setting the inside edges against sliding downhill. Your knees will have to come together somewhat to do this. Put your poles towards your back. First bring one ski up a ways directly in front of where it was. Do that with the other ski. Continue, alternating. This is for slopes medium in requirements between diagonal and sidestep. It is tiring.

Instruction

If you're seriously interested in style, particularly racing style, it might be wise to ask if your instructor is certified. Two organizations give certification in New England—The United States Eastern Amateur Ski Association and the Professional Ski Instructors of America. There's an amusing minibattle going on between these two outfits over Nordic teaching standards. Both, however, have high standards; the Professional Ski Instructors reputedly have the highest.

I wouldn't introduce kids to touring, by the way, by sending them to lessons. They could be made to think that touring was work if they immediately were put under the guidance of one of skiing's drill instructors. It might ruin the fun, the spontaneity of the thing.

A *half-herringbone* is less tiring, and can check you on many slopes when your diagonal begins failing. Instead of gliding one ski forward, simply herringbone it. You'll want to herringbone the ski on your downhill side.

DERRIÈRE TECHNIQUE

Do not be afraid to fly by the seat of your pants, so to speak. On a steep run, especially down a twisting and turning logging road, it

Herringboning.

would be better to sit down and drag your hands (gloves) than zoom into the birches. You can control yourself in almost any situation this way. It's fatiguing and especially hard on the hands. It's easy to ease into a controlled fall by sitting down, but you may go into an uncontrolled fall when you hit a series of bumps. Straighten up a bit for them.

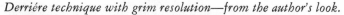

Derriére technique with grim resolution—from the author's look.

EGG

For fast downhill schussing. Bend the knees. Lean over and put your elbows on your thighs. Cuts wind resistance.

EXTRAS

WEDELN

Yes, you Alpine hotshots, you can parallel on touring skis. You need more angulation, since it's more difficult to carve without steel edges and when the heel is free. Now you know where Stein Erikson got his style.

SKATE TURN

Recall the step turn. When you step off, push back against the other ski. That is the skate turn. Just a power version of the step turn. Repeat with the other foot to continue skating. You can skate easily on cross-country skis, they're so light.

CHANGEUP

It is simply a way of varying the pace while climbing. As you go uphill, drop the arms to the side and take about three quick steps, on your toes, taking a deep breath, straightening up. Resume diagonal. Refreshed.

TELEMARK

This is a beautiful old-fashioned turn. It was the rage 60 years ago. It is rarely used in New England because it requires powder snow. Nevertheless, it can be accomplished on crust covered with only a few inches of powder.

It's simple in theory, but it demands good balance. Here's how: Extend one leg forward, bending the knee, of course, in the process. Extend it far forward, so the other leg trails behind with the knee almost touching the ski. This is the true Telemark position, used by ski jumpers to stabilize themselves upon landing. Steer the forward ski towards where you want to go, keeping your weight distributed equally on both skis, and the trailing ski will follow. Lift your arms up for balance.

THE WARREN DANIELL SURE-FIRE METHOD FOR SERENELY COASTING DOWN NARROW, ICY, STEEP WOODS ROADS IN NEW HAMPSHIRE AND ELSEWHERE

Cross-country skiing is not always easy. There are humbling moments. Surprisingly, these generally occur when you're going downhill. You can set your pace when striking uphill—at, say, a crawl if necessary. But it's remarkable how the slope can slip away from you on a downhill run—until, as you rocket across the crust with the wind getting louder and louder and the slope steeper and steeper, you perceive that certain hollowness in the stomach which the generations of man have recognized as one thing: fear.

It is at this point that you are faced with skiing's existential question: to turn or not to turn. In fact, you realize you should have faced up to this question earlier. If you had, and opted for neat linked traverses, you wouldn't be going so fast.

If you are in an open area, the dilemma easily resolves itself. You turn, catch an edge which you fleetingly wish were steel like that on a proper ski for going downhill, and fall flat on your face, soon skidding to a stop. Or you decide to grit it out, get going insanely fast, catch a tip, and fall flat on your face, not so soon skidding to a stop. Since you don't have those downhill skis on, all you have to do is pick up your pride and proceed—instead of investigating for broken bones.

It is when you are going lickety-split down a narrow, curved, steep, icy logging road and the like, however, that the situation becomes more complicated, if not downright dangerous. Such situations are not uncommon in New England, especially when snowmobiles have preceded you and packed the snow into a beautiful bobsled run. In touring there is no ignominy, of course, in taking off your skis and dragging your hands.

But now there is another way out. There is a way to coast happily down the iciest, steepest woods road with restrained speed and a dry bottom. It was invented (some say reinvented) by Warren Daniell, a good friend and skiing companion who was a four-event skier in the class of 1920 at Dartmouth. Warren, now retired and living in Hanover, was for many years chief engineer at the huge Great Northern paper mill in Millinocket, Maine, and he has put his engineering genius to work to devise this sure-fire method of solving one of ski touring's central problems. Warren has been skiing all his life, but he found it necessary to turn his thoughts to this predicament only a little while ago, after he had turned 70. He didn't enjoy falling as much anymore and felt that sliding on his rear was undignified for a man his age.

Here's how it works: When you get going too fast, put your ski

Warren Daniell.

poles together between your legs and ski on them. Ride them down the hill. Snowplow or bank around the turns. The more you scootch down on them the harder the tips will dig in and the slower you'll go. It really works, although you might feel wobbly the first couple of times. There's only one catch: Don't try to use bamboo poles or you soon will be riding two splintered sticks. You have to use metal or fiberglass poles.

Great ideas are always simple.

By the way, you can also hold your poles to the side (grasping one hand near the baskets) and drag them. This is a more conventional way of slowing down.

IN ADDITION

· You can kick turn over fences. Be careful over barbed wire.

· Don't look at your ski tips. Ancient Eastern Wisdom: Widen your perspective.

· More Ancient Eastern Wisdom (Down East version): Don't fight the slope or the snow or yourself. Accept it all.

Waxing

LET'S PUT 70 per cent of the waxing information you need for New England touring into one brief paragraph:

Rub green hard wax on your skis when it's quite cold and the snow is powdery. When it's not so cold rub on blue hard wax right over the green. When it's icy crust scrape off the hard wax and smear on—you'd best be indoors so it'll smear—sticky blue klister wax, using the heel of your hand. Use wax remover to take if off when snow falls again.

See? Waxing is easy. But it would be downright disgraceful to stop here. What about protecting your ski bottoms in some way? Complications, complications.

THEORY

Snow is composed of crystals. Under most conditions these crystals have jagged little arms. When you have wax on your skis these little arms stick up into the wax. This is why waxes will give skis a quality of sticking on the snow—"grip" it's called, or "purchase." You will grip even when you're going uphill. This miracle of cross-country skiing—skiing uphill—is mainly due to waxes. But partially due to technique: Often you don't get much grip unless you keep zipping along, giving your skis little opportunity to slide backward, and you are balanced on them properly.

Perhaps the real miracle of cross-country skiing, however, is that with the same wax you not only get grip, but when you exert force to move forward, you move forward. You slide; "glide" is

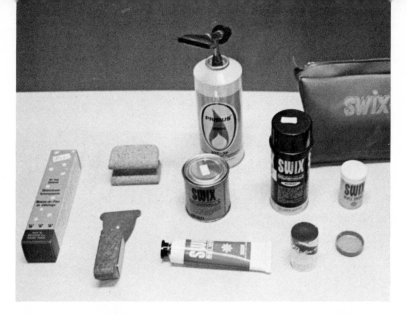

Bottom, left to right: wax remover, scraper-cork, tube of klister, hard wax with cap off. Top, left to right: cork, burn-on base wax, torch, spray base wax, wax kit, hard wax with cap.

the term most often used. This is because heat from friction between the wax and snow surface creates a miniscule layer of water for the skis to glide upon. When you slow down or stop, the layer of water disappears and the jagged little arms of the snow crystals stick once again into the wax. This sticking momentarily occurs when you push off during the cross-country stride. "Setting" the ski, which a skier may do when he climbs uphill—that is, pushing it down into the snow more—serves to get more grip, to get those jagged little arms into the wax. So you see, waxing and technique are well intertwined.

One more thing: Snow varies greatly in its structure, especially with the passage of time. New dry snow has very jagged crystals and easily penetrates into wax. For this reason a hard wax is needed. With a soft wax, there would be such a marriage between wax and snow that you'd be stuck in one spot—indeed, wax and snow would freeze together.

As snow gets older, the crystals melt slightly and lose their jaggedness a bit—or they may melt a lot if the temperature rises a lot. Thus a softer wax is needed to make it easier for the wax and our famous "jagged little arms"—which are now becoming rounded with melting—to stick together.

Finally, when the snow has melted on the surface (the moisture acts as a lubricant), a very soft wax is needed. When it has melted and then refrozen into ice or crust, a soft wax is also needed, one with super-stickiness, since it has to deal with few "jagged little arms" at all.

BASES AND BINDERS

Base wax is put on skis to protect the wood from moisture, and, it is claimed, to provide a better adhering surface for running wax. I know successful racers, however, who don't use base wax. They are fearful of its stickiness. They feel that if their running wax gets run off, they will have the snow sticking to base wax, and this will slow them down. Also, since the debate whether modern, laminated skis should be kept dry or wet has not yet been resolved, I'm somewhat unconvinced of the necessity of keeping out moisture from the bottom of skis. A lot of people are worried that their skis will get too dry.

What's a beginning tourer to do? I suggest base waxing your skis, although I wouldn't worry about it too much. There may be something to the idea of preventing moisture from soaking into the bottom of the skis and freezing. Racers' problems with base wax stickiness will rarely be yours.

Base wax is usually a pungent, brownish substance. Tar compounds are best. The traditional way to put it on is to burn it in. This means you spread it on with a brush and use a propane torch or similar device to boil it briefly—bubbles appear—as you wipe off the excess with a rag. Be careful not to char your ski bottoms.

Many people object to the use of a torch, which costs only a few dollars and should be equipped with a fan nozzle. A lot of people don't like to use fire, and they particularly object to their kids burning down the house from the basement up. These people,

Burning in base wax.

then, should not buy a torch—although it's handy in other waxing situations, as we will see—and instead should get paint-on-and-let-dry base wax or the new spray kind. These are quick, although you have to let all base waxes set awhile (check the directions). But they don't last as long as the burn-in variety.

With factory-new skis, be sure to take off the coat of varnish before you apply the base wax. This can be done with sandpaper. It's an easy job. Don't take off a lot of wood unnecessarily. If you're an average tourer you may only have to treat your skis with base wax once or twice a season. All other waxes, of course, should be removed before putting on base wax. Don't put base wax (and be very wary about using heat) on synthetic surfaces. Follow the manufacturer's directions closely.

Binders, often also called base wax, are waxes put on between the base wax and the running wax. They provide a better base for the final or running wax to stick to. They come in hard wax tins or soft (klister) wax tubes. They work, especially when it's icy and wax tends to wear off fast, but few tourers use them. They're a refinement. If you're a beginner forget about them until next year.

HARD WAXES AND KLISTERS

Terminology varies with each wax manufacturer, but generally "hard" waxes come in little tins and "klisters" or soft waxes come in squeeze tubes. Some quite soft waxes, frequently called "klister wax," also come in tins.

Hard waxes are used for snow that has not melted or refrozen. Klisters are used for snow thus metamorphosized.

Waxes are color-coded, and for the most part the biggest manufacturers—Swix, Rex and Rode—have the same colors for the same kinds of wax. As the wax goes from hard to soft, from wax for cold snow to wax for warmer snow, the main colors go from cold to hot—green, blue, violet, red.

SELECTING THE WAX

Almost everybody uses a waxing chart. We have reprinted here the Swix chart because Swix is the largest seller of waxes in the world. Or read the labels on the wax cans. That's what Bob Gray, our best racer, says he still does.

The important thing is "reading" the snow so you can use the chart correctly. This means not only determining what the snow is like at present, but what it'll be like where you'll be later in the day. Will the weather warm up during the day? Better take a softer wax in your pack. Will there likely be powder beneath the trees when you reach deep woods in an hour or two? Maybe you had better put a layer of blue on your skis for that powder and only a patch of blue klister beneath each foot for the icy track you'll be on until you reach the woods.

Several factors traditionally are used for a snow reading: temperature, moisture content and type of snow—new, old, and coarse-grained, which includes ice and crust. Moisture and temperature are pretty closely interrelated. As it warms, more crystals melt and

✳ New Snow	✳ Old Snow Corn Snow	⬡ Rough Corn Snow , Ice
SPECIAL GREEN 18°F AND COLDER	**SPECIAL GREEN** 10°F AND COLDER	**BLUE KLISTER** BELOW FREEZING ICE AND CRUST
GREEN 18°F TO 27°F	**GREEN** 10°F TO 21°F	
BLUE 27°F TO 32°F	**BLUE** 21°F TO 30°F	**VIOLET KLISTER** CRUST AND WET SNOW FROM 25°F TO 37°F
VIOLET FREEZING TO THAWING 32°F	**VIOLET** FREEZING TO THAWING 32°F	
YELLOW KLISTER WAX SOGGY SNOW SLIPPING TRACKS	**RED** SOGGY SNOW	**RED KLISTER** WET OR SOAKING-WET SNOW
YELLOW KLISTER WET SNOW	**RED KLISTER** WET OR SOAKING-WET SNOW	

the snow gets wetter. The temperature can be read from a thermometer, preferably one placed on top of the snow, but the temperature of the air can be used. If you don't have a thermometer, use the moisture test: If it's hard to make a snowball, the snow is dry and it's usually cold. If it's slightly moist, then you're around the freezing point. If it's wet, it's warm. Quite obvious.

The type of snow is also easy to determine. It, too, is closely related to the temperature—the history of the temperature. New snow is new snow. Powder that's been around a few days, especially with temperatures above 20 degrees and the sun shining, is "old" snow. Coarse-grained snow has melted and refrozen (although it may once again be melting).

Next, read the chart. (Each wax manufacturer has a chart.) Or read the labels.

HOW TO APPLY THE WAX

For hard waxes, simply peel back the lead foil and crayon the wax on. A thin layer works best. The thicker the wax layer, the more it will behave like the next softer wax. Use this to your advantage when conditions warrant it. And you'll want a thicker layer if you think the wax will wear fast. After application (it makes no difference in which direction you rub), smooth the wax down with a cork. Don't smooth it down, however, when you want it to behave a bit softer. See how many variables you can play with?

You can put hard wax on outdoors or indoors without difficulty. You can even paint it on from a can or pot by heating it and using a paint brush (but this is really unnecessary).

Soft tin waxes and klisters present more of a problem when you're outdoors. Indoors you can just daub a thin strip down the length of the ski and use your hand to smooth it out. Unless it's fairly warm outdoors, you'll need some kind of heat source. There are many special devices sold in ski shops, but I prefer the inex-

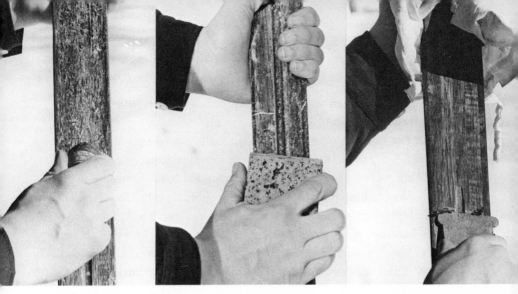

Applying hard wax, left to right: crayoning it on, corking it in, scraping it off (author just happened to be holding cloth).

pensive propane torch, which works better than butane at low temperatures. Heat the tube, daub the wax on, then heat it on the ski and spread it out with your hand or paint brush (natural bristle, which burns less readily). If you want, you can use the heat and paint brush technique indoors, thereby keeping your hands clean. If you use your hands, you can clean them with petroleum jelly. You can heat the klister in a can and then paint it on. This

Applying klister, left to right: squeezing from the tube, smoothing it out, getting a sticky hand.

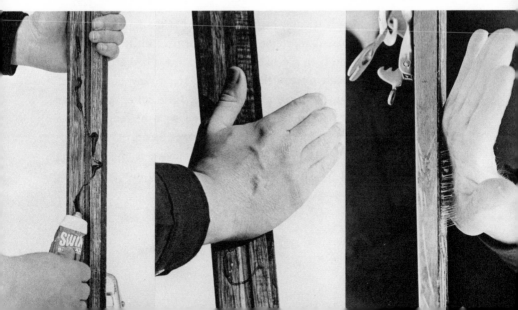

is excellent when you want to try mixing klisters and when you have several pairs of skis to wax.

The center groove of the ski is usually waxed with the running wax—or paraffin to prevent it from icing up. Since it is not always being rubbed along the snow it is more liable to ice up.

Skis should be as clean and dry as possible when waxing. The important exception to this is that you can put a softer wax over a harder wax. And sometimes you can temporarily put a harder wax over a softer one. At least you can mix it into the softer wax. Wet skis are hard to wax. Use a torch to dry them if you have to. You can use a torch also to take off old wax. Heat the wax and wipe it off with a cloth. Or you can use some of the paste or spray wax removers. Many solvents such as paint thinner will work just as well.

Skis just waxed should be allowed to cool outside before they are placed on the snow. Otherwise, they will ice up. Don't judge your wax job until you've skied a few hundred yards at least.

Stick with one firm's waxes if you're just starting out. Soon you will be experimenting with many others and developing your own personal expertise. Complications can be fun. There's nothing quite like being the only person to wax right for a difficult day.

NEW ENGLAND WAXING

The problem with waxing in New England is the famous changeability of weather. A morning wax will not necessarily be the wax for noontime and both are likely to be wrong for late afternoon.

The best idea is to wax harder if you are in any doubt about future conditions. You can always daub a little softer wax under your foot to get more grip or put the softer wax the length of the ski over the harder one. So take a few waxes along.

Thirty-two degrees Fahrenheit and just above is the irritating area for waxing. Often the best answer here is to mix waxes. I've had very good luck mixing red and violet in various proportions under foot, with blue the length of the ski. Develop your own system.

Real wet snow is common in New England. The waxes for this —yellow, red, and yellow, red, violet and silver klister depending on the brand and other factors—work to some degree, but I'm still waiting to find the tourer who doesn't occasionally find himself hopelessly sloughing through the mush, a foot of snow caked beneath each ski bottom. They say if in complete despair take all the wax off and slap on paraffin, which doesn't ever ice up. This is difficult to do, however. Another suggestion: Don't lift the skis off the snow. And keep moving.

To take off wax in such circumstances, and in others—such as when the temperature drops and it starts snowing and you've got to take off your red wax quickly—you need a scraper. A putty knife will do or a razor blade (but be careful). There are special scrapers.

MORE COMPLICATIONS

I know a racer who claims waxing isn't important at all. The whole thing is technique, he says. If you're slipping on a hill, ski harder, he says. Maybe that's why he loses so often.

But waxing really isn't that important for the average tourer. Despite trying to avoid it, I see I have gotten enmeshed in some complications. As I indicated at the outset of this chapter, several waxes will be all that's necessary for most days. Blue, green, and blue klister will cover just about every condition below freezing. Some violet and red to fool around with for borderline conditions aren't really complicated to use. In the spring get some red and violet klister. Start with a couple of waxes, learn to use them well, and then move on to others.

In General

YOU CAN ski practically anywhere. All you need are a few inches of snow. This is a major claim of cross-country skiing which commercial interests have begun trying to disprove, for obvious reasons. Partially they are right: The easiest skiing requires maintained trails, and most people like an atmosphere which the banks of the Charles River in Boston might not provide and which the Trapp Family Lodge supplies in spades.

But, essentially, that famous go-anywhere claim is right. Some people don't mind a little more variable skiing, which striking off down an unmaintained woods road might provide. And it might provide adventure, tranquility and a three-mile downhill swoop. Some people can't get to the mountains every weekend. So they try to see what fun can be found in their city park or suburban reservation—there is plenty to be found. There is even plenty of fun to be had simply by laying out a track in the field in back of your house. It won't be much of an experience in the way of exploring, but since skiing's pleasure comes partially from the joy of the body in motion, that can be enjoyed anywhere.

You can ski in the middle of some of New England's cities— mainly in parks. To boggle the minds of friends and strangers, wait until a real snowfall stops traffic, and, while everybody else is digging out or staying home, calmly ski to work or school. This would be possible much of the year for country kids in northern New England. Tony Clark of the Blueberry Hill Farm touring center in Brandon, Vt., is working with the local school system to get physical education credit for students who ski to school.

In the suburbs, touring opportunities are plentiful: watershed reservations, Audubon Society sanctuaries, abandoned town roads, bridle paths, power lines, large fields, trail bike paths, etc.

In the country, touring is limitless: woods roads and logging roads, snowmobile trails, unmaintained dirt roads, abandoned railroad rights-of-way, lakes, rivers, hiking trails, fire roads, and so on. Many trails will not be skiable, however. Inquire with rangers, at general stores and post offices. You'll find many that are—and don't be too quick to believe the warning of some old codger around the cracker barrel who may think you're slightly touched if you want to ski *uphill*. The best way of finding out what's available is to use a topographical map, which can be purchased at many sporting goods stores. A list of sources of trail information is in the Appendix. The Appalachian Mountain Club and other hiking clubs put out excellent maps.

If you're willing to bushwack, you literally can go anywhere. Some people even prefer this kind of skiing.

Then of course there are those maintained—and unmaintained but mapped—trails of the ski touring centers, inns and of downhill areas beginning to cater to the ski touring crowd. In the following pages I have focused on these places to some degree because many people like to go to them, and because these places provide trails and facilities that can be, well, pinned down. It would be impossible to describe all the woods roads in New England, but I think I have pinned down most of the specific ski touring areas in our region. I've also included directions towards other kinds of touring experiences available to the more adventurous.

This section is biased towards places I've been and places I've liked. The emphasis is on northern New England because this is where most skiing is done—this was true particularly during the past two poor snow years.

It should be kept in mind that the ensuing pages were written in the spring of '73—based on a winter-long series of journeys around the region. This is such a fast-growing sport that names, places and fees change very rapidly. So don't be too surprised if fees during the winter of '73–'74 are higher than I've stated.

Maine

ACADIA NATIONAL PARK, MOUNT DESERT ISLAND

THIS IS probably the most beautiful place to ski in the whole of New England. Many of the millions who have visited Mount Desert Island in the summer must have wondered what it was like during the winter, when the crowds have disappeared and the pink granite of the mountains has been draped in white. It's magnificent. I'm prejudiced, of course. I was born there.

The only problems are weather and snowmobiles. As along the rest of the New England coast, the sea is a moderating influence, and snowstorms inland are frequently rainstorms on Mount Desert. Never *assume* there is enough snow for skiing. Make sure by calling the national park office (207–288–3338, 8 a.m. to 4:30 p.m.).

Unfortunately, all the unplowed park roads open to autos in the summer are for snowmobiles. Trails for skiers and snowshoers have been set aside, but the machines have the lion's share of the park, including some of the "carriage" roads which are not open to cars in the summer, and some of the more scenic routes, such as the Cadillac Mountain Road, Ocean Drive, and the carriage road around Eagle Lake. Perhaps if more tourers visit the park the snowmobiles might have a few routes taken away from them.

More and more people on the island are turning to touring. A small group, some associated with Bar Harbor's world-famous Jackson Memorial Laboratory, a cancer research institution, have been striking off into the mountains for years. Now the new ecology-

The skier had better be prepared for icy winds on the Cadillac Mountain Road. In the background, Frenchman's Bay.

oriented College of the Atlantic, also in Bar Harbor, has many avid tourers, and the school is talking about laying out a race course. One of the places where students practice their touring is the Kebo Valley Golf Course on Bar Harbor's Eagle Lake Road.

The State of Maine is trying to bring tourers to Mount Desert. The Department of Commerce and Industry has arranged a package with Delta Air Lines. For $30.50 per person for two nights you can stay at the Atlantic Oakes motel, part of the old Sir Harry Oakes summer estate next to the Bar Harbor terminal of the Nova Scotia ferry "Bluenose." This includes ski equipment rental.

That is the de luxe way, however. There are several motels and inns on the island where you can stay for far less, down to a few dollars a night per person. Only one place, the Cranberry Lodge in Northeast Harbor, has meals, but there are homey little restaurants in each of the villages. I recommend Mitchell's Lobsterman Restaurant, West Street, Bar Harbor—all the fish you can eat for $1.25 on Friday. Grocery stores and a couple of small supermarkets are open in the winter, as well as a beer joint in Southwest Harbor. The Cranberry Lodge has a bar.

If you prefer winter camping, you can do that at the Black Woods Campground. Inquire with the park service (Acadia National Park Headquarters, Bar Harbor 04609).

The Oakes ski equipment comes from Bob Chaplin, 18 Roberts Ave., Bar Harbor, who sells and rents a line of Bass gear from his home. Also, in Northeast Harbor Holmes' Store has been renting and selling equipment.

A trail map is published by the BAR HARBOR TIMES, 66 Main St., and it is printed in a brochure containing much valuable information for tourers, such as suggested parking areas. A better trail map to the island is the Appalachian Mountain Club one, but the TIMES map is invaluable because it shows which trails have been reserved for snowmobiles. You can pick it up day or night in a big box outside the park headquarters in Hulls Cove on Route 3 in Bar Harbor.

The touring routes are 20 miles of a handsome network of carriage roads weaving through the park. You can travel from Northeast Harbor north around Parkman and Sargent Mountains to Eagle Lake and then back via a different road. Much of the way Somes Sound will be visible; it's the only fjord on the East Coast. Another trip might take you from the parking area at Jordan Pond (beside the celebrated Jordan Pond House) up along a cliff overlooking the pond to a grid of carriage roads at the west of Eagle Lake. Another network is met going from Jordan Pond south past Long Pond to Seal Harbor and the sea.

There are many roads that will take you to sites where the blue, cold, white-capped ocean and the numerous islands will appear, and many others that will bring you to the white-sheeted lakes cached among the steep small mountains. The island is a masterpiece of glacial sculpture, and it's a display case of flora and fauna even in winter. Watch for bald eagles. Although much of the park was severely burned in a 1947 forest fire, trees have returned, and the original spruce, fir and pine still stand in many places.

Snowmobiles are not permitted off their routes, but skiers are, although in many places, because of the rocky nature of the island, it's rough going. But it's worth it, especially to reach a summit of one of the many mountains. At least for a few feet you'll have to take off your skis and climb, but no climb is very arduous.

Eagle Lake in February. The lake is surrounded by mountains.

Cadillac is only 1532 feet in elevation, but its practically straight up from the sea. On a windy day the exposed slopes present a danger of frostbite. I'm probably going to get in trouble by suggesting a snowmobile route, which the Cadillac Auto Road is, but it's worth whatever difficulties to get to the top—for the most heady view in New England. Those snowmobiles have to be respected, though; it's their highway and they roar around corners at 30 m.p.h.

I'm not going to write about the butterflies in my stomach when I think of the beauty of the island in the winter, of sailing alone down a carriage road or sharing a lunch with a friend while overlooking the ocean. I'm not going to write about the special, unearthly peace of the whole island in this season, the way the snow looks on rocks leading into the sea, the sight of an osprey soaring over bare hills, the warmth and quietness of the small stores and lunchrooms. It's so remote in winter that for many people it seems the end of the world; it was the beginning of the world for me. The island seems to inspire books, not paragraphs, so I don't feel like trying to even suggest its beauty in this brief space. Many have written books about it. Maybe someday I'll write mine.

SUGARLOAF (NEAR KINGFIELD)

Sugarloaf is Maine's great downhill ski area. Some of the qualities which have contributed to its unique appeal as a downhill resort— its remoteness, its wilderness situation—contribute also to its value as a place to tour.

"People can tour much nearer their home," says Sugarloaf general manager Harry Baxter. "This is a service for people who're already here. When it gets too cold and windy on the mountain, they can go touring." It must be some indication, then, that touring is catching on with the downhillers, for Baxter has had to hire one full-time touring instructor and three part-timers. These people mainly deal with ski weekers who get a day of touring as part of their total instructional package. The day includes a wine and steak meal at the Red Stallion Inn. Baxter has equipped the ski shop with, naturally, Bass gear (Bass is a Maine firm). All the skis are mohair. Skis, boots, poles rent for $5.50 for the first day, less the succeeding days. Equipment sales and rentals are also available in ski shops in the area.

Despite Baxter's disclaimer, some people—mainly Mainers—do go to Sugarloaf just to tour, and the main attraction is the wilderness—specifically, Bigelow Mountain. This is the bare, blue mountain across the way from Sugarloaf. It dominates the northern horizon as you look out from the top of the lifts. It is Maine's third highest mountain (after Katahdin and Sugarloaf), and some compare it to Katahdin in grandeur. Baxter has had laid out a fantastic nine-mile N.C.A.A.-quality trail which climbs up Bigelow

Sugarloaf instructor Ralph Ferguson skiing up an old logging road on the side of Bigelow Mountain

a good ways. I skied on it with Ralph Ferguson, one of the part-time touring instructors. Ferguson, 30, had recently quit life in Greenwich, Conn., to reside in a cabin by the Carrabassett River "where in the spring I can catch trout from my backyard." Ferguson peeled off his ankle-length fatigue coat (very chic in the Sugarloaf area) and we struck off up a rolling trail that had a few inches of fresh powder on an ample base—at a time when the rest of New England was nearly devoid of snow.

It was an exhilarating afternoon: As we would zing around a corner, we sometimes would catch sight of the impressive Sugar-loaf snowcap to the south. At other times we would notice only birch and spruce and ski tips furrowing through clean whiteness. By some standards the trail wasn't maintained very well (this year they will be getting a track sled). It would be demanding for many tourers, but it was the kind of semiwilderness touring which Maine has in great potential and which I consider the best of all possible touring. The route was an old logging road for much of the way; other old logging roads (most of the land is owned by paper companies) led off around the mountain. They pleaded for exploration, but explorers had better be somewhat knowledgeable in the ways of the wilds; it's rough country, and the next plowed road could be scores of miles away.

There are several other trails maintained by the ski area (26 miles in all). One parallels the Appalachian Trail for a few miles; another is a four-mile jaunt near the base lodge. A very fine one is on the right-of-way of the extinct Sandy River narrow-gauge railway from the old Bigelow station house seven miles to Carrabassett Village, a ski town which was only a few A-frames 10 years ago. As you drive to Sugarloaf along the Carrabassett, watch for tourers on this trail on the other side of the river. When you see them effortlessly double poling along, you'll resolve to try it. It's a gentle downhill all the way.

The trail map is free. One needn't be dependent on Sugarloaf to enjoy the Sugarloaf area. Other trails will turn up with a topographic map and a little exploration.

I learned to ski Alpine at Sugarloaf. Although it has gone bigtime since, I still think of it as one of the few Alpine areas left worth skiing. Even the aprés-ski life is far friendlier and less plastic than at many resorts. The whole atmosphere of Sugarloaf, Carrabassett and Kingfield is, I suspect, what Aspen was like in the old days, or Stowe. It's another good reason to go there if you're a tourer, and think how much cheaper it'll be than downhill skiing! (But, sadly I must report there aren't any real cheap places to stay anymore.)

SQUAW MOUNTAIN, GREENVILLE

Sugarloaf is on the edge of the semiwilderness, but Squaw is close to the *real* woods, the fabled Maine woods of Thoreau which extend for 100 miles nearly unbroken into Canada. In fact, Thoreau used Greenville as a jumping-off place for one of his excursions. Greenville is still a rugged logging town, although it has become much more of a summer resort since Thoreau's day.

Most of the wild land in Maine is owned by paper companies and Squaw is no exception. The resort was started from scratch several years ago by Scott Paper, and the firm is anxious to develop it into a big, four-season place. Ski touring, as at Sugarloaf, is seen as an adjunct to the downhill area, hotel, restaurants, etc.

"We're trying hard to find ways to make money from it," Bruce Taylor, Squaw's public relations man, frankly says of the touring facilities. "But it's hard. It just isn't lucrative." The way they make money now is by renting equipment ($5.50 a day) and offering lessons ($4 per person in a group, the same as Alpine lessons). Like Sugarloaf, Squaw offers a day of touring for its ski week people, complete with lunch at Mountain View, a former loggers' provision farm three-quarters of a mile from the Squaw lodge.

They're always thinking: Taylor and Chip Howe, the touring instructor, both mentioned the possibility of instituting trail fees. "Grooming is expensive," Howe said. (They have a trail grader and track setter and are proud of their grooming.) "Maybe we'll have mandatory check ins and check outs," Taylor said. "Some of the things people try to escape by ski touring will come to an end as touring becomes more popular."

Despite this money-grubbing attitude, I enjoyed touring at Squaw. First, it is more remote than Sugarloaf and far less developed, and yet it has an abundance of luxuries such as sauna, heated swimming pool, fancy bars. This isn't particularly my preference, but because of the lack of crowds and the casual atmosphere I found these pamperings quite appealing. Perhaps, though, only because Scott Paper paid for them.

The countryside is the main reason I enjoyed Squaw. A few minutes striding will take you into authentically wild woods. Chip, Andy Szelenyi and I spent a few hours one misty afternoon hiking two miles up to Moose Point, where you get a good view of 40-mile long Moosehead Lake on a clear day. (With the right snow conditions, you can ski on Moosehead.) On the way, passing through trees thick with rime, we came across the tracks of two moose—broken only that morning. Chip should know. He was born in Greenville and has been in the woods all his life. For a hobby he goes trapping. Chip, 21 years old, lithe and affable, raced for Greenville High School when there was a ski team. "Now they're into snowmobiling so much," he said, "the team has died." He is trying to revive it.

Snowmobiles weren't to be seen on that day, but Chip admits the "buzz freaks," as he calls them, can be a problem. The resort caters to them, ringing up 20 per cent of its hotel sales from snowmobilers shelved in a bunkhouse at Mountain View. The major problem is that snowmobiles have to use the ski touring trails immediately around the lodge. Squaw works hard to keep them otherwise off ski trails, and the touring routes are attractively well marked.

There are 30–35 miles of touring trails (a crude map of some of them is available) and many logging roads through some of the nicest forest land imaginable. But it's roughly $15 to $30 a day per person for a double room at Squaw.

ANDOVER

People perusing the Ski Touring Guide may wonder why there are so many trails listed for the little town of Andover (pop. 791), located in an untouched mountain valley in Oxford County about 20 miles northwest of Rumford.

Frank Akers, proprietor of Akers Ski of Andover, put them there. Andover is one of Maine's most important ski towns, particularly in cross-country skiing. Indeed, the whole of northwestern Maine—the Oxford Hills, an extension of the White Mountains—has for a long time vied with southern Vermont as a producer of top cross-country and jumping competitors.

Akers, 37, is a blue-eyed, blond-haired stocky fellow who looks like a Swede but whose accent tells you immediately he was born in Maine. He started his business in 1958 as a adjunct to ski coaching and teaching at nearby Mexico High School; in 1962

Frank Akers in his ski shop.

he imported only 50 pairs of skis; now he works full-time to
bring in 2000-plus a year and is a major supplier to high schools
and colleges around the country. With the touring boom he has
seen his business shift considerably away from racing. At this mo-
ment, his shop is the only solely-Nordic ski shop in Maine.

To visit his impressive, tasteful showroom in a converted stable,
with its ash walls and colorful rugs, is to see that he has pros-
pered from skiing. From conversations with coaches and dealers
I found that he is universally respected as one of the fairest individuals in this particular business. Akers has spent a good deal of
time attending to the development of scores of miles of trails in
the hills that ring Andover, and has even bought land near his
shop to lay out a well-maintained small network for customers
and townspeople, especially the local school kids.

Many of the kids belong to the Torger Tokle League (up to
13 years old). One day I went skiing with some of them, Akers,
and Frank Morgan, 67, one of the league's coaches. Morgan, who
was an official at the Squaw Valley Olympics, related that the
town has been ski crazy since 1926, when he helped found the
Pineland Ski and Outing Club, still in existence. It hosts races
drawing competitors from around New England and, occasionally
in the past, around the world. Morgan had little difficulty keeping
up with us through the stands of pines on a snowy, quiet day.
He showed us the new lean-to shelter built for the kids, where
they come sometimes to picnic. Many of the parents are getting

into touring, he said. "It's something both kids and parents can do together."

Next year ('73–'74) Akers may have rentals. He says he hasn't really tried to get people to come to Andover to ski, but he has been describing trails and giving maps to more and more people, and is more than happy to continue to do so.

Andover is the kind of place where you can go skiing from the main street or someone's backyard. The spectacular mountains (up to 3000 feet) around the town are easily accessible, though there are many demanding trails, especially near Grafton Notch and Baldpate. At 1800 feet the village itself is picturesque, and has a green with a bandstand near the town hall and church. In short, it is one of the finest little towns in Maine, and the skiing is superb. There are few accommodations, however, and I believe the only restaurant is a funky down-home lunchroom. But, dear reader, should you always have to accept the same, sterile motel rooms and overcooked expensive steaks? Bah! Try a place like Andover, which really isn't a resort at all. There are many villages like this all around New England.

RUMFORD-MEXICO

Another historically ski-mad community in northwestern Maine comprises the twin paper-mill towns of Mexico and Rumford. The Chisholm Ski Club was formed there in 1923 and at one time the area had the largest ski jump in the eastern U.S. The F.I.S. cross-country world championships were held there in 1950. The area still produces a fair share of the Nordic national team.

The club has the Chisholm Winter Park on Black Mountain in Rumford, with three jumps, a T-bar and cross-country trails. Club president Tom Arsenault invites tourers to use the daily-maintained, wooded and open country three- and five-kilometer courses, used also by the local high school teams. A map is available at the ski lodge.

SUNDAY RIVER INN, BETHEL

Sunday River is a relaxed, family-oriented, small ski area near the New Hampshire border. It's only natural that touring would appeal to the kind of people who go downhill skiing here.

Touring started about five years ago at the ski area proper. Now it is centered at the Sunday River Inn, a family hotel on the access road a few miles outside Bethel. There are about 20 miles of trails groomed twice a week with a sled. Instruction is given by the Inn's touring director, Andy Wight. Rates are $4 a person in a group. Rentals are available and so are sales. Snowshoes, too, are rented. A trail map "contribution" is 10 cents. Several clinics are held each year. In the near future, from the signs of interest, the whole town may be skiing, and a town-wide network of trails is being planned. Kids in the elementary schools tour for phys. ed.

The Sunday River Ski Club sponsors races "for every age and ability." Last year a very successful one was held on March 11. This will become an annual affair. The good snow cover of this portion of the state—it is also in the Oxford Hills—is a major advantage to touring here.

The Inn, where rooms are $12 per person for a double including breakfast and dinner, is renowned for its simple, delicious food prepared by Peggy Wight, Andy Wight's sister-in-law. One newspaper cuisine reviewer spent $19 for *seven* people, four kids and three adults. The place goes to great lengths to make kids feel at home.

OTHER AREAS

The 25 state parks are officially closed in winter, but the unplowed roads and paths heavily trodden in summer make excellent touring routes. Write the Department of Commerce and Industry, State House, Augusta 04330, for a brochure describing them. The most famous park, *Baxter,* where Katahdin is, has unmatched touring; a trip there is described in the chapter on mountain touring. Another park with excellent touring potential, virtually untried as yet, is *Camden Hills,* where fine views of Penobscot Bay are to be found. The *Camden Snow Bowl* downhill area has indicated an interest in developing touring. *Grafton Notch State Park,* between Upton and Newry, includes part of the *Appalachian Trail,* which has many skiable portions in Maine. This area has already been mentioned in connection with Andover's ski trails.

The extension of the *White Mountain National Forest* into Maine has skiing opportunities, but most of the best possibilities, such as the unplowed Route 113 from Gilead to North Chatham, have been pre-empted by snowmobiles. (Although it is possible to ski on 113.) Check with the ranger in Bethel for details on touring this area.

Farther south near the New Hampshire border, *Fryeburg,* home of Fryeburg Academy, has eight miles of trails. City parks are used in *Portland* and *Lewiston-Auburn.* Auburn was the home of John Bower, the country's greatest Nordic combined star, winner of the Holmenkollen in Norway.

The *University of Maine Forest* in Stillwater is used by students. There is available a three-and-a-half mile course run by University racers. South of Bangor, at *Bald Mountain Ski Area* in Dedham, there are about five miles of trails leading from the lodge to Goose Pond.

Other ski areas reporting several miles each of touring trails are *Lost Valley* in Auburn; *Mt. Abram,* Locke Mills; *Evergreen Valley,* Lovell; *Big Rock,* Mars Hill; *Burnt Meadow,* Brownfield; *Caribou Ski Slope,* Caribou; and *Colby Ski Area,* Waterville.

Rangeley has a Nordic ski club and several cross-country ski shops—that is, people selling equipment out of their homes. The annual Rangeley Ramble is sponsored by the club. It's a 10-kilometer open race held in January.

Don't forget, for the really adventurous, there's the whole north woods. What about doing the Allagash on *skis?*

New Hampshire

JACKSON

JACKSON VILLAGE, set in the magnificent Mount Washington Valley 10 miles north of North Conway, is New England's first ski touring town. The whole community has given itself over to the ski touring boom, and a couple of years has produced the most extensive cross-country area this side of Scandinavia—75 miles of trails.

The organization guiding this development is the non-profit Jackson Ski Touring Foundation, established with $30,000 supplied by local businessmen. The foundation maintains trails ($15,000 spent for this the first winter), provides rescue service, handles publicity, runs the local school kids' cross-country program, schedules the shuttle bus and generally administers touring activities. It is headquartered in a new, wooden building in the center of town. The building also houses a cross-country ski shop and ski school run by the Jack Frost Shop, whose downhill ski fashion center is located next door.

Other local businesses handle the rest of the commercial aspects of the sport—food and lodging. Cross-country ski packages are offered in the brochures of places like the Dana Place, Christmas Farm Inn, Wildcat Inn & Tavern, etc.

People using the Jackson trails, which are public, are asked to join the Jackson Ski Touring Club at $5 for individuals and $9 for families (plus a $1 initiation fee). If they don't join, they are asked to "contribute" 50 cents a day if adult, 25 cents if children —for which they get a fine trail map.

The trail network offers an amazing variety. There are a num-

Jackson village and, beyond, the beginning of the Presidentials.

ber of constantly and professionally groomed runs in the immediate area—indeed, it is possible, as in Andover, Maine, to simply step out of your backyard—or your hotel's backyard—and take off. There are also less regularly maintained and more challenging trails leading up to the flanks of Mount Washington, whose summit, 12 miles north, dominates the northwestern sky. Three local ski areas, Tyrol, Black Mountain and Wildcat, have cooperated with the trail system. There is a trail leading to the base of each, and one leading away from the top of each area's lifts.

A particularly exciting trail, I am told, is a 10-mile run from the top of Wildcat down to Jackson. Most of this trail goes through the White Mountain National Forest. Many other trails are in the national forest; some go to shelters it is possible to use for overnights. The Jackson system ties in with the Appalachian Mountain Club trail system, and thus there is an almost unlimited scope to ski touring adventures in this area. I think it would be easily possible to ski from Route 2, say at the entrance to the Evans Notch Road—across the border in Maine—over to Wildcat, down to Jackson, and then perhaps all the way across the Kancamagus Wil-

Trail grooming at Jackson

derness to Waterville Valley, which is developing an extensive network, too—a distance well over 50 miles.

I visited Jackson several times last winter and was invariably pleased by the Nordic atmosphere of the whole community—people actually using skis to get from one place to another—and the particular friendliness of the efficient little touring center run by Avery Caldwell, 26, and Jack Lufkin, 25, both from Rumford, Maine. Both had raced for Rumford's Stephens High School and in college. Jack was on the '68 Olympic team.

The center is always busy, with beginning ski touring classes conducted on the town green right outside, and Jack told me they rent 200–300 pairs of skis a day on weekends. Full equipment rental is $5 a day; group lessons are $4.50. The shop will also hard wax your skis for 25 cents and put on klister for $1.

Jack said the townspeople have been quite happy about embracing ski touring. It's brought a lot of business. The citizens have responded by contributing to the foundation in many ways, some providing, for instance, emergency phones in homes near trails. The preparations for any trauma are impressive. Emergencies are rare in touring, but some of the country near Mount Washington can get rough. There is a rescue patrol; first aid stations—mainly, caches of supplies—are all over the area.

The shuttle bus running from North Conway to Wildcat with many stops in-between is a convenience. This makes it possible to ski a long distance one way and get wisked back quickly on the bus at the end of the day.

There is a wide range of prices in the lodging and alimentary scene, though once again no real cheapies. Most of the people who stay here are from the Boston area. Many of the day trippers, however, are young folk employed at the neighboring downhill areas.

APPALACHIAN MOUNTAIN CLUB

The A.M.C. hut system is deservedly famous. It is the only one of its kind in North America. In the summer it is possible to hike the length of the White Mountains staying at the nine huts. No need to bring sleeping bag or food. Blankets are provided and good grub is served, complete to a trail lunch. At last this European-type chain of huts is coming alive in the winter, thanks to the demand created by ski tourers.

One hut, at Zealand Falls near Crawford Notch, was open all last winter, and two—Zealand, and Carter Notch, near Wildcat— will be available to tourers and snowshoers in the winter of '73–'74. Perhaps these openings presage a fully-operating hut system in a few years, such as exists in the winter Alps and Scandinavian hills. One major difference, however, between the A.M.C. winter huts and European huts and for that matter the A.M.C. summer huts: In winter you have to bring sleeping bags and food. But bunks are provided and there is a gas stove to cook on.

Andy Szelenyi and I visited the Zealand Falls Hut last spring. We parked our car at 4 p.m. one cloudy day at Zealand Campground on Route 302 and headed up a road which was only lightly covered with snow and was obviously asphalt underneath. A few miles of not being able to get your pole points to stick can be very tiring. (The same thing happens when you're poling on ice on a lake.)

We were glad to have the trail leave the road. But we immediately were confronted with a raging stream, which we had to take off our skis to cross. This was required at several other places up the hard-to-follow route, which meandered through groves of young pine. Several times when we attempted to cross streams with our skis on we got them wet and the water froze to the bottoms. The trail became particularly difficult as darkness approached and we found we had to traverse a swamp which was beginning to come unglued. These difficulties might sound formidable, but they weren't. It was splendid wild country.

Well after dark we finally got to what we thought was the neighborhood of the cabin. We had also finally lost the trail, and the map didn't seem to be much help. Thus we were relieved to see suddenly a light glimmering on a mountainside.

Chris "Hawkeye" Hawkins, 20 years old, the hut's caretaker, was surprised to see us straggling in at such a late hour. It was only a seven-mile jaunt, but we were plenty tired, and we welcomed his offer of hot tea. The hut was quite luxurious: a big, old wooden place with framed mountain photographs on the walls, warmth gushing from a new wood stove and a gas wall heater, a big kettle of water ready for more tea, and lots of books and magazines we later perused. "Get all the reading done you ever want to do," Hawkeye remarked. That night we slept in one of the two unheated four-tiered bunkrooms off the main area. We were the only guests.

In the morning we were treated to a view out the windows we hadn't expected. We were indeed on a mountainside (altitude 2700 feet) and could look down Zealand Notch for miles to see Mount Carrigan at the edge of the Pemigewasset Wilderness. The east side of the notch was scree dusted with snow. A nineteenth-century logging railroad track cut across it. This would be our route out.

Hawkeye told us that even though on weekdays the hut was often empty, on weekends an average of 20 people would be staying there, mostly ski tourers. Reservations through the A.M.C. Pinkham Notch Camp were technically necessary, "but it really hasn't been necessary this year." (Hut capacity is 36. The charge is $4 a night.) There hadn't been any tragedies with the tourers although a couple of people had frozen some extremities. Hawkeye, trained in first aid and well supplied with equipment, had treated and returned them to civilization.

As we left the hut, Hawkeye was going to Zealand Campground to pick up supplies dropped there by an A.M.C. truck. A big, blond, talkative fellow, he seemed to like his job. He communicated by radio daily with the Mount Washington Observatory and had a little pocket radio he carried outside in case he broke a leg. "But it doesn't work most of the time," he said.

We headed south down the notch trail, then turned east towards Ethan Pond and emerged at Willey House on Route 302 right in the middle of Crawford Notch, eight miles from Zealand Falls and about nine miles from the car, which we had to hitchhike to. The Ethan Pond Trail is part of the Appalachian Trail and not ideally suited for tourers—poorly marked, no bridges across streams, and there is one hell of a sharp downhill run the last

Hawkeye starts his hike to civilization to pick up supplies.

mile to the notch. But we enjoyed the challenge. Earlier in the
season, with more snow and well-frozen streams, it would have
been easier. The feeling of remoteness was with us constantly.

We look forward to skiing into the Carter Notch Hut. It's less
remote, only four miles from the upper gondola terminal at Wildcat, where you can connect to the Jackson-developed trails. But the
scenery is especially rugged there and it's 3450 feet high.

Besides skiing to the huts, there are numerous touring trails
maintained right around the Pinkham Notch Camp on Route 16.
They range from easy to very difficult. The lower part of the
Mount Washington Auto Road is recommended after a light
snowfall before snow machines pound it into ice. Fabled Tuckerman Ravine can be approached but not safely skied upon until
late spring, when actually it becomes an Alpine area without lift.
The most famous late-season skiing in the East is here. The Tuckerman Trail can be ascended by tourers, but should not be de-
scended, due to the danger to those coming up. You can, however,
ski the 2.5-mile John Sherburne Ski Trail from the vicinity of
Tuckerman down to the notch—if you have some skill. This whole
area can be quite tricky, especially in inclement weather. A number of people have died skiing on Washington, a good percentage
from avalanches. Checking in and checking conditions with the
Pinkham Notch Camp is mandatory. Get a map there, too, and a
trail description pamphlet.

If you've never visited it, you'll find that "Camp" is something
of a misnomer for Pinkham. There's a big A.M.C. office, family-
style dining room and bunkroom-hotel, all open to the public. It's
best described as rugged luxury. (Adult lodging $6, supper $4,
breakfast $2.) Pinkham Notch Camp is a New England tradition
and should not be missed. It offers cross-country skiing weekend
packages including lodging, meals, waxing and equipment lectures,
technique demonstration, a movie, and an all-day tour for a very
modest fee. You must, however, rent or buy your equipment elsewhere. Eastern Mountain Sports in nearby North Conway is where
most people go, or to Jackson.

WHITE MOUNTAIN NATIONAL FOREST

Both Jackson's and the A.M.C.'s ski touring opportunities are largely in the national forest, as are many ski trails of Waterville Valley.

These trail networks do not limit what skiing there is in the 730,000-acre tract. There are approximately 1200 miles of hiking trails in the forest, many suitable for touring, many too rugged and rocky. The national forest management is doing maintenance work on some of the trails with the winter hiker, snowshoer and ski tourer in mind.

Any trail is open to tourers, but it should be realized that with one exception, snowmobiles may use any trail, too. Under presidential order, national forests must regulate off-road vehicles, but as of now only the Mt. Washington Carriage is closed to snowmobiles.

The A.M.C., the U.S. Coast and Geodetic Survey, and the national forests all have maps. I prefer the plastic-coated A.M.C. ones.

The White Mountains Ski Touring Club (c/o White Mountains Region Association, Lancaster 03584) puts out a mimeographed "Evaluation of Ski Touring Trails." It relates several trips starting from the majestic east-west Kancamagus Highway, for some years now open in the winter. One route leads on the Greeley Ponds Trail from the Kancamagus to Waterville Valley, six miles away. There are also several trails mentioned in the Gorham area.

WATERVILLE VALLEY

This huge downhill ski area, started only a few years ago in an isolated valley by Tom Corcoran, Olympic skier and friend of the Kennedys, has become a chic success. Its recently initiated ski touring program is also a success and one of the more advanced in New England.

It's run by Don Johnsen, who once skied 450 miles along the

The shape of the future? No, the shape of the present. Waterville Valley's touring center is one of many in New England.

Continental Divide in Colorado. Johnsen is assisted by several full-time instructors who dispense teaching-tours at $4 for a couple of hours, $7 for a 10 a.m. to 3 p.m. tour. Rentals are $5 for the first day, decreasing thereafter (mostly excellent Asnes skis and some mohair). Ski weekers can tour instead of tackle Mount Tecumseh on downhill skis.

"This is a low-key operation," Johnsen told me as we watched some off-duty Alpine instructors race around the track outside his touring center. "But we want to make it as professional a service as possible without lapsing into what Alpine has become."

It is a service largely for those who come to Waterville Valley at least partially for its array of saunas, bars and expensive restaurants and are a little bored or frustrated with Alpine skiing. As Harry Baxter said of Sugarloaf's touring, it's a service for people who would go there anyway. However, last year this kind of touring attracted thousands, and hundreds and hundreds of lessons were given. Johnsen talks of expanding.

The 35-mile trail network will perhaps be expanded to 70 miles by the time this book is published. This is what Waterville has really got going for it: rolling terrain, fields, large forest expanses, shallow and steep grades, primitive and well maintained trails. Outside the immediate area it's all national forest. The trail web is well marked. A map sold at the touring center costs $1, perhaps a portent of things to come. "There is no charge for the use of our trails at this time" is printed darkly on it. Johnsen says trail fees are being considered.

Waterville Valley is getting into the open or "citizens" race scene. The first annual Derby was held last February with 120 competitors off in a mass start around a 10-kilometer course, with an oom-pah band to set the rhythm.

Although it's a playground for the affluent, Waterville is offering touring for local kids at a nominal rate and free to a retarded children's school. These programs are starting to sprout at many touring centers in New England, a phenomenon which needs to be encouraged.

HANOVER

Hanover is the home of Dartmouth College, one of the top skiing schools in the world, and it is only natural that touring is highly developed in the area. For instance, Dartmouth offers touring as part of its "ski rec" physical education. (Touring competes, however, with three Alpine skiing areas owned by the college: a golf course, a hill and a mountain.) Dartmouth racers have 10 miles of track to practice on and this year a lighted track for night skiing. The Nordic squad at the college has always been strong.

Most important to ski touring, Dartmouth has the Dartmouth Outing Club and its chain of cabins and 120 miles of trails. The town has a large touring populace which is constantly charting trails, holding clinics, swapping stories.

The D.O.C.'s cabin and trail system is famous. Although the college does not maintain touring trails as such, it invites tourers to use the routes, which include 70 miles of the Appalachian Trail, many sections of which are ideal for touring. The college's part of the Appalachian Trail runs from New Hampshire Route 112 near Mount Moosilauke, which the college owns and where it has a lodge, all the way across the Connecticut River to Barnard Gulf on Vermont Route 12. The trail goes from the White Mountains to the Green Mountains. Maps and trail descriptions can be obtained from the Director of Trails and Shelters, D.O.C., Robinson Hall, Box 9, Hanover 03755.

The D.O.C. has recommended the following routes: west on the Appalachian Trail or Tucker Trail from Norwich to Happy Hill cabin and beyond to West Hartford; north from Hanover to Harris junction on Moose Mountain and then over the mountain; the Appalachian, Quinttown and Clark Pond Trails in the neighborhood of Smarts Mountain; and the Moosilauke area.

The trails are available to the touring public, and the Appalachian Trail is theoretically free of snowmobiles—although not in fact—but the large, comfortable, D.O.C. cabins are another story. Except for emergency use, the college prefers you reserve them (it charges for them). It isn't terribly enthusiastic about noncollege people filling them up.

The Hanover Conservation Council, filled with ardent ski tourers, has produced a map showing Hanover's trails and unmaintained roads. Many of the trails are up and down Moose Mountain, which dominates the eastern half of town and where John and Mary Clarke have the Moose Mountain Cross-Country Lodge (Etna 03750). One of the trails is practically in downtown Hanover—from Occom Pond it runs north through a fine grove of tall pines along, on one side, the Connecticut and, on the other, a golf course.

While at Dartmouth I hiked the back woods of Hanover and have skied it many times since. No more gentle, typically New England land could be found. Another reason for skiing in this

A fine trail along the Connecticut River in Hanover. Only excellent swimmers should try to ski on the river ice here.

area would be to taste Hanover life—perhaps a concert in the Hopkins Center, a stroll around the campus, an investigation of million-volume Baker Library, a lunch in the Hanover Inn. I think a taste of Hanover is essential to the New England experience.

OTHER AREAS

Touring is more developed in New Hampshire than in Maine, so I won't list all the downhill areas that have some kind of touring set-up. Most do. And the bigger ones have bigger set-ups—*Cannon Mountain,* for example.

North Conway is promoting skiing in the Whitaker Woods and surrounding area, where there are 15 miles through beautiful pines. Some trails lead past an old granite quarry and there are fine views of Mount Washington. A brochure with map can be picked up almost anywhere in North Conway—at Eastern Mountain Sports, for example.

A highly unusual cross-country program exists at tiny *Canaan College* in Canaan. In order to help its finances, the school has gone commercial. For a fee, it will pick you up at the airport, put you up at the college, give you an environmentally educational experience and teach you touring.

Franconia Notch State Park has a fully developed trail system, over five miles on logging roads and old Route 3. The park is just off Interstate 93. Snowmobiles are not permitted. Try other state parks. There are trails, for instance, in *Pawtuckaway State Park*—between Manchester and Portsmouth.

Also in the southern part of the state: The *Wapack Trail* is skiable—21 miles from Ashburnham, Mass., to Greenfield, N.H. Numerous trails exist on *Mount Monadnock* in Jaffrey. The old town roads of *Acworth* have been much skied upon. *Mount Cardigan* has many trails, some made for skiers, others for hikers. The A.M.C. has a lodge here open only to members. There are cross-country ski resorts at *New Ipswich* ("Windblown") and *Grantham* ("Grey Ledges"). Peter Davis, a U.S. Cross-Country Ski Team racer, runs the Pole and Pedal Shop in *Henniker,* where he rents and sells gear, and there are miles of trails beginning at the shop.

Excellent field skiing is known all along the *Connecticut River Valley*—areas off Route 145 in Clarksville, Stewartstown, East Columbia and East Lancaster, for example.

Way up north, besides touring at the *Wilderness* downhill area in Dixville, it is possible to ski in the real wilderness of the *Second College Grant* near the village of Wentworth Location. It's a whole township owned by Dartmouth. Contact the College Forester, Hanover.

The Office of State Planning of the State of New Hampshire (State House Annex, Concord 03301) is scheduled to issue a report on state trails, including an inventory of ski touring trails, in 1973. This might prove valuable.

Vermont

TRAPP FAMILY LODGE, STOWE

THIS WAS the first New England recreational center devoted to ski touring. Now all of six years old. It's also the biggest touring area in terms of business—600 to 700 people on a weekend day are not unusual, according to Larry Damon, touring director.

The lodge, perched on one of the foothills of Mount Mansfield, is run by Johannes von Trapp of the "Sound of Music" family. It is large (135 rooms), Tyrolean in design, luxurious and expensive (single with bath, $25 a night). Damon, a dark, quiet, former four-time American Olympic team skier, said the touring business is what fills the lodge every night.

The Trapp touring experience is unlike any other in New England. It is *crowded* in a way reminiscent of downhill resorts. Trapp is located at the biggest downhill resort area in the East.

People crowd into the deluxe ski shop, where several of Damon's 14 instructors (count 'em) are likely to be selling gear, several others adeptly waxing skis for small fees, and several outside in a big field will be instructing. Lessons were up 300 percent in '72-'73 from the previous year. These instructors might include one or two of the three Norwegians Trapp employs. One of them is Babben Damon, Larry's wife, who was a member of the 1968 Norwegian Olympic women's relay team, which won the gold medal.

Beyond the field are about 40 miles of trails, including a network around the lodge which probably provides the best groomed routes in New England. Grooves for the skis are set, making it immeasurably easier for the beginner.

The ultimate in touring luxury.

There were plenty of novices around on the day I skied two and a half miles up to the Slayton Pasture cabin, where a caretaker stays during the day dispensing hot drinks and wax. (The cabin is also available for sleeping-bag overnights.) It was a day of pleasant gray light, gentle snowfall and a path through birches and fir. It was also a day of patiently waiting for others to move along in the track, and, on the way back, of worrying if there would be others in your way as you zoom down—but the crowds thin out in late afternoon. The ride down in that excellent track was thrilling. Actually, moving along with everyone earlier wasn't really an unpleasant experience. There is a conviviality to tourers, even beginning tourers. Frankly though, this kind of touring wasn't my cup of cocoa.

It might be yours, however. For a beginner willing to spend the money, this would be just about the best place to learn. Damon has hired the best when it comes to instructors. The instructional attitude is relaxed, and he sells the best when it comes to equipment (Norwegian). "The books all make touring sound too complicated," he said.

"A Telemark? What's a Telemark?" asked Babben. "Nobody

in Norway uses a Telemark anymore." The set tracks are the best possible conditions for practicing the stride. There also are many trails interesting to the experienced skier.

The Trapp trails connect to the many other touring trails in the Stowe area. It is possible to ski around the side of Mount Mansfield to Underhill, then down the 12-mile Madonna Vasa cross-country race course to the Madonna ski area. It is also possible to ski 12½ miles overland to the Bolten Valley downhill area. This is termed an expert trail and Larry said he hoped to have a cabin for overnights about eight miles out. There is a $1 trail fee which includes an excellent map.

It is possible, too, to ski down to the Mansfield access road, cross the road and ski over to the Trapps' *second* ski area, Edson Hill Manor, where there is another shop. Yes, they are successful.

NORTH AMERICAN NORDIC SKI TOURING CENTER, STOWE

(AND JAY, KILLINGTON, MT. SNOW AND MANCHESTER CENTER, VT.; FRANCONIA, N.H.; WILLIAMSTOWN AND HOLYOKE, MASS.; GRANBY, CONN.; AND CHESTERTOWN, ALLEGHANY AND KEENE, N.Y.)

(AND NOW, WISCONSIN, MINNESOTA, COLORADO, WYOMING, IDAHO AND CALIFORNIA.)

It had to happen. Ski touring had to go corporate big-time sooner or later, and North American Nordic, with its ever-expanding list of touring centers and products, was there first (only last year). A purist friend disparaging calls North American Nordic "the Howard Johnson's of cross-country skiing." Although the standardization is unappealing, as is the slickness ("Have We Got A Sport

For You!" declares one of their brochures), on the whole I find
them of excellent quality in instruction, equipment and management; they are convenient (often located on golf courses); the
prices are no higher than at other places; and they are possibly
doing more to promote the sport than any other entity except the
Ski Touring Council.

Stowe is the headquarters, where John Greene and Joe Pete
Wilson, both former U.S. National and Olympic Ski Team members, preside over their empire. Joe Pete is also coauthor with
William Lederer of a very successful book on cross-country technique.

Greene wrote me about their philosophy: "We have now completed our first year of operation and feel very confident about the
future of Nordic skiing in this country, and the soundness of our
concept . . . .

"Our approach was to establish areas where virtually every as-
pect of ski touring was offered. Secondly that every North American Nordic Center offered the same facilities, products, service and
level of expertise as any and all other North American Nordic
Centers. . . ."

Many felt that North American Nordic must have overex-
panded disastrously for a poor snow year. When I visited the centers in Massachusetts and the one in Connecticut, nary a tourer
was to be found. The ones I visited in Vermont didn't seem to be
that busy, although I hit them during weekdays in lousy snow
times. Perhaps, however, their overhead is such—they usually rent
space in a lodge or golf clubhouse—that they don't need hordes
to do a good business. They are more enjoyable to hang around
in than many of the busier touring centers at downhill areas.

The staff is young, hip, talkative and casual, yet competent.
Real high-class ski bums. (I am not using the phrase pejoratively.
I used to be one myself.)

The equipment is good: Bonnas and Splitkeins, mostly. And
some mohair Skiloms. The instruction is not high-pressure; I saw

one area manager talk somebody *out* of a lesson. Yet instructors are all certified. There's a complete repair shop.

The trails are well prepared. The networks are usually not large but this is not always true: At the Mountain Meadows center in Killington, miles and miles of logging roads and fields can be used. There are crude maps, and no trail fees.

The rates won't bust you—$5.50 rentals, $4 group lessons. Accessories such as back packs, clothing, books and other items are sold.

And there are all sorts of extras: Daily tours at 1 p.m.; guided picnic tours; numerous clinics covering all the basics; a Ladies Day; NASTAR amateur races; moonlight tours; free coffee; cross-country ski week packages offered with the affiliated lodges. The center in Williamstown had a well stocked bar (and a blaring TV set).

They are great places for beginners, for those who have an hour or two to tour and for those who want to be sure they're getting top quality. That standardization is quite complete, as can be gleaned from my generalizations about the areas, but there are differences—in personnel and mainly in trails. References will be made to several of the centers elsewhere in this Where to Ski section. The prospective North American Nordic customer should be aware that some of the centers may change location. Write to the office at Stowe, Box 1308, Zip 05672, for a brochure.

OTHER STOWE AREAS

Stowe and its vicinity is rivaled only by the Mount Washington Valley in the extent of its ski touring opportunities. Besides the Trapp and North American Nordic areas, John Handy, headmaster of the Stowe School, has laid out a number of trails which connect to the Edson Hill Manor area run by the Trapps. Better check the status of these trails with Edson Hill. They may be restricted.

In addition to the Madonna Vasa Trail and the Bolton Valley Trail, which link up with a Trapp trail at Nebraska Notch, there are numerous paths on and around Mount Mansfield and Spruce Peak. They connect with the ski lifts. The Mansfield summit trip is a long-revered route. From it you can get a good view of Lake Champlain and the Adirondacks on one side, Mount Washington and the Presidentials on the other. Check with the downhill ski areas for information on these trails.

Bolton Valley, a downhill resort you reach via road from Waterbury, teaches cross-country and maintains 25 miles of trails. It's only a dozen miles from Stowe across the mountains, but 30 miles of driving.

The Farm Motor Inn and Country Club, just north of Stowe on Route 100, is promoting touring. There's a lot of rolling, open country there. In fact, in every direction there's a lot of open country suitable for touring. It's probably the easiest region to tour in New England. The Ski Hostel Lodge in Waterbury Center, seven miles south of Stowe, puts up tourers, and its owner, Martha Guthridge, who has to be one of the most delightful hosts in Vermont, is knowledgeable about touring in the area. You can drift back into the hills for miles and miles. Or try skiing from there to Stowe. Lovely country. Don't worry about skiing on somebody's land unless you see him with a shotgun. Try to avoid skiing through backyards—although the most typical reaction to this would be to invite you in for a hot drink.

BLUEBERRY HILL FARM, BRANDON

This is It. This little-known inn hidden way up in the Green Mountains north of Rutland is my choice for Best Touring Spot in New England. It's uncommercial, relaxed, small and comfortable. Don't all rush there, however; it's almost always booked up. But day skiing is available.

Let me be a little more specific about Blueberry Hill's charms. Six years ago Tony and Martha Clark bought an old (1813) seven-bedroom house at the edge of the national forest near Brandon

Gap. Tony, 29, a bespectacled Englishman born in France who used to teach in Massachusetts, had been skiing for years, and soon the Clarks and friends were using the fields and old roads and trails surrounding their home. They took in guests in the summer and a couple of years ago decided to spur on their winter business by promoting what they had been enjoying privately, ski touring.

The Clarks turned an old blacksmith's shed into their ski shop, with ornate pot-bellied stove, stumps and tractor seats to sit on, and a pot of free soup warming on the stove. They hired a boy to wax the skis and a couple of instructors for the weekends, and their friends, who turned themselves into the Vermont Ski Touring Club —now headquartered at the farm—cut trails in the summer. *Voilà!* A touring area.

It's this casualness which helps create the special atmosphere there. Here is Tony's attitude toward the sport:

"In touring you need a *guide* in the woods, not an instructor to stress technique. I wish more places like ours would open up. I basically feel you can't combine downhill and touring. At Killington they're just out to make a buck.

"To me this is just a way of living in Vermont. I know what my limits are. I'm certainly not going to get rich on this. But at Killington they just want to pack in people and make them pay 50 cents for a cup of coffee."

Soup's on at Blueberry Hill.

Another part of the appeal of Blueberry Hill is due to the hard work of Martha, who presides over the elaborate farm kitchen, where on a big black stove she fixes gourmet dinners. People feast and talk for hours. The menu might be tomato soup, pork roast, lemon potatoes, green beans, flaming royal peaches, cheese pie—all for $4.50. In the morning: homemade coffee cake, eggs and bacon, waffles and sausages. Much of the food is organic, and most is produced on the farm.

The skiing here is good, too. Over 40 miles of trail, much through the Green Mountain National Forest, including some miles of the Long Trail and an eight-mile jaunt to the Middlebury Snow Bowl. The Clarks have another inn, the Churchill Ski Touring Center, a few miles away down on Route 73, connected to Blueberry Hill by an easy trail. The trails are unmaintained except by skiing and snowmobiles, but they are surprisingly well maintained nonetheless, and Tony thinks people like a little variety in trail conditions. "Half the joy in touring is setting your own track." I skied on a few trails and have no complaints. The shop sells Bonnas and rents them for $6 a day. Double rooms, by the way, are $12 to $15. Quite reasonable.

There's a big race in March, an end-of-the-season fling called the Pig Race. At the finish of the seven-mile run, open to one and all—it attracted 250 the last time—everybody sits down to pork from a whole pig roasted on a spit. The man who comes in first wins a bottle of homemade blueberry wine; the first-place woman gets a blueberry pie. The race and roast have already become famous in central Vermont.

There is something almost indefinable about the Blueberry Hill aura. Possibly it's the Clarks: young, in tune with their environment, not corporate money-hungry. Possibly it's the way they've artistically fashioned their place to be so pleasing to the senses— the smell of soup on the stove, the sight of hand-hewn timbers and unpainted wood, the sounds of happy kids (the Clarks have two of their own). At Blueberry Hill, too, you feel part of the community, something many of us have lost in contemporary times. Blueberry Hill's guestbook is a loom upon which you can weave a short pattern of your own design and colors. There must be something symbolic in that. Tony is right. There should be more places like his.

WOODSTOCK SKI TOURING CENTER, WOODSTOCK

Going into its fourth year of operation, the Woodstock Ski Touring Center is the Rockefellers' contribution to cross-country. It is owned by the impressive 111-room Woodstock Inn, a "Rock-resort," and as might be expected, the touring center is a well-run, luxurious place.

You reach it by turning off Route 4 and going down the west side of the village green in this neat, handsome, rich town. Go past the big, white Inn and a quarter of a mile down the street is a snow-covered golf course and clubhouse, which in the winter is the touring center. At last a winter use has been found for all those golf clubs in New England!

I was greeted by Laszlo Peri, the touring director, who poured

me a glass of wine as we talked about Woodstock touring. Peri is a dark, thirtyish Hungarian who lived and skied for years in Norway and is a Norwegian-certified instructor. According to him, the growth of the center has been phenomenal. "We are mobbed," he said.

Even on the extremely poor snow weekday when I visited the center, there were numerous people skiing and an equal number loafing around the shop, which was well-stocked with Norwegian gear and provided tea, coffee, boullion and chocolate bars. There is also a large rental shop ($4 half day, $6 full day). Instruction is provided by Peri and three others at $4 a group session.

Much of the instruction is given right out the door on the golf terrain. There is a series of trails around the course and in the lightly wooded hills of Woodstock's outskirts. A legible map is available.

These trails are easy and not lengthy, Peri said. He also gave me a map of the Sky Line Trail from Woodstock to Barnard. This nine-mile route goes from the Suicide Six ski area, three miles north of Woodstock in South Pomfret, to Hawks Hill in East Barnard. It is privately maintained and well marked.

Peri puts on guided picnic tours a couple of times a week for $3 a person. You can bring your own lunch or the club bar-restaurant (open noon to 2 p.m.), will prepare one for you, complete with glug. Moonlight tours are also held. There are Nordic NASTAR races (the first one in the East was held here in 1971) and a fair number of weekend touring clinics. Woodstock is one of the few bigger touring resorts not to charge a trail fee nowadays. Not bad at all for the Rockefellers.

LONG TRAIL FOR SKIERS

In 1969, two friends—Daniel Pennie and Andy Szlenyi—and I spent 14 days in January and February skiing the length of Vermont, going from the Massachusetts border in Guilford to the Quebec line at Richford, a distance of slightly over 200 miles.

We did it mainly for the usual reasons which can be subsumed under the phrase "for the hell of it," but an additional reason was to establish a route which we hoped would become a Long Trail for Skiers, running generally to the east of the famous hikers' Long Trail (which can be skied in certain sections).

It was a beautiful trip—the beauty of winter in Vermont. On sparkling, snappy mornings we would slice down narrow logging roads, not knowing what was around the bend. We would steam across field after field in the afternoon sun to take a break—chocolate bars, raisins—on the warm tarpaper roof of an abandoned chicken coop half-buried in the snow. We skied down frozen lakes in the moonlight. We skied on everything: fields, roads, trails, railroad tracks, and there was plenty of bushwacking. There were few specifically touring trails then; we had to find our way by guesswork.

There were anxious moments: On the first day we got lost, saw each wax job wear off quickly on the icy crust, and wound up bone-weary at dark in somebody's backyard 17 miles from where we started—but six miles from Putney. John Caldwell was going to put us up for the night at the Putney School. We ignominiously completed the day's planned distance in his car. But the next morning, after a little help with our waxing from Bob Gray, we were back where we had left off, determined to ski all the way.

One afternoon while skiing across some hilly fields near Waterbury, Andy fell and badly cut his face on the crust. That was quite a day all-around. Twenty-two miles through frozen rain. All we saw was white snow or gray clouds. Andy had fallen because he had misjudged the slope in the flat light. Another day, the last, we skied most of our 23 miles in a heavy snowstorm. Fortunately, much of the route was a ski tourer's superhighway, the Hazen's Notch Road, a state highway closed in the winter.

Mostly, though, there were good feelings. Like the people we met and the places we stayed. Warren Chivers, an Olympic skier of the '30s, put us up in the gym of Vermont Academy in Saxtons River. Another ski coach, Tom Bryant of the Sterling School in Craftsbury Common, found beds for us in the school's infirmary. Another teacher at the school, Stephen Wright, a transplanted Georgian whose wife fed us grits and Mayhew preserves for breakfast, skied with us for a morning. We never unexpectedly encountered another ski tourer during the whole trip.

Most nights we stayed in youth hostels. They provided us a great opportunity to keep our living expenses below $75 apiece. That's right. That's what we spent for two weeks of skiing in Vermont.

Not long after our trip I sent our marked topographical maps to Vermont's state forester, who said he was definitely interested in establishing a skiers' Long Trail. The north-south trail idea is still very much alive, and the state is developing trails on its own land with this goal in mind. However, private outfits are doing much of the development—the development not only of a north-south trail, but of a trail system throughout the whole state.

We had been too modest in our hopes. The whole state may soon become a Long Trail for Skiers. Already it is possible without much difficulty to ski for scores of miles from touring network to network. For example: it is possible to ski from the Jay area trails—probably 100 miles of them—to Montgomery Center, then down the Hazen's Notch Road to Lowell, on to the Madonna area, then to the Trapp trails at Stowe, over to Bolton Valley, then via Camel's Hump to Mount Ellen (an area the state is developing). From the trails in the Glen Ellen-Mad River area you can ski onto the Sugarbush trails (40 miles of them). Then down Route 100 or through the mountains to Bread Loaf and the Middlebury Snow Bowl. A trail from here to the Blueberry Hill Farm in Brandon is maintained. It's an easy ski from Brandon to the *Mountain Top Inn* trails in Chittenden.

Continuing south, there are the Killington trails and the unplowed road from North Shrewsbury to Round Top Mountain.
Then Okemo, which is developing its touring program. There are
several touring centers in the Londonderry area. Farther south there
are the Stratton trails—one to Stratton Pond. Then down past the
Somerset Reservoir to Mt. Snow, then to Wilmington on Route 9.

Well, by gosh, that's the length of Vermont. All pretty much on
good trails. And think of all the traverses of Vermont to be made.

Youth Hostels

These are the kind of places cross-country skiers naturally gravitate toward: inexpensive (nonprofit), homey (nonplastic) inns where you
sleep in bunks and cook your own food in a communal kitchen—or in
some cases, for a small fee, can opt for a hearty meal served family-
style. They are not restricted to the young, and all you have to have for
entrance is an American Youth Hostel pass, which you can get at any
hostel. The pass also admits you to hostels in 47 other countries.

There are 35 youth hostels in New England, 12 of them open during the winter. Many have touring trails right outside the door. (Indeed, AYH is promoting touring as the ideal complement to what it
promotes in the summer, bicycling.) The overnight fees run from
$1.50 to $3.

There are winter hostels in South Waterford, Maine; Danbury, N.H.;
Craftsbury Common, Lowell, Richford and Rochester, Vt.; Hyannis,
Littleton, Martha's Vineyard, Pittsfield, and Sunderland, Mass.; and
Lakeside, Conn.

For the latest *Hostel Guide and Handbook,* write American Youth
Hostels, Inc., National Campus, Delaplane, Va. 22025. Copies are
$1.50 apiece, including postage and handling. The guide comes free
with a hostel pass, which costs $5 for those under 18, $10 for 18 and
over, and $12 for family membership including children up to and in-
cluding 18 years. Write to the same address.

There are what many people would term disadvantages to hostel-
ing: no alcoholic beverages; lights are out often at 10 p.m.; hostelers
are expected to share in cooking and cleanup duties; and "houseparents"
may wake you at 7 a.m. From my experience the observance of all these
rules has been pretty loose.

OTHER AREAS

As is evident from the above few paragraphs, Vermont is easily the best developed state in New England when it comes to touring. Nearly every downhill area has touring, and there are more cross-country shops, each with its own mapped trail system, than I can keep track of. Let me simply list a few more good areas to look for touring:

One of the places we skied on our length-of-Vermont journey has been turned into an official State of Vermont ski touring system. This is at Granville Gulf State Reservation on Route 100. The *Puddledock* trails provide about three and a half miles of good skiing. If you are heading south from Warren, after about five miles watch for the Puddledock Road parking area on the left. There is a box with maps inside, and the trails are marked with what is becoming the official Vermont ski touring trail symbol—red, metal rectangles.

The *Sugarbush Inn* has the Sugarbush cross-country business. All the amenities. This is extremely typical Vermont countryside: woods and fields and stone fences and old barns. One of my fondest touring memories is a swoop down a gigantic field near Sugarbush to have lunch inside an abandoned barn as the snow fell quietly outside.

It may seem I have a vendetta with *Killington*. It's a convenient symbol of downhill excesses. I could rage also against Stratton, Mt. Snow, etc. But Killington is providing a lot of people with touring fun. The woman who runs the touring show there, Janice Fleetwood, is very experienced in touring in the area.

Burke Mountain near St. Johnsbury is another downhill area offering the full range of touring activities and facilities. The trail system in the coming year will be expanded to 32 miles and there's a cabin on one trail for overnights. Clinics will be held weekly.

The *Swedish Ski Club* in Andover (between Chester and Weston) is an old-time area. There are 20 miles of trail loops. No accomodations or other facilities.

A misty day after a snowstorm in the hills off Route 100 near Pittsfield, Vt. Notice the house in the background.

The *Merck Forest* in Rupert has 2600 acres and many touring devotees. The trails are jeep roads. Snowmobiles not allowed.

South Londonderry has *Woody's Cracker Barrel Ski Shop,* run by Woody Woodall, one of the pillars of Vermont ski touring. Fifteen miles of trails. In Londonderry there's the *Viking Ski Touring Centre.* Thirty miles of trails. One trail leads along the West River to the quaint town of Weston, where the Markham House is specializing in feeding and lodging tourers.

The state puts out a ski touring brochure, and the Ski Touring Guide is exceptionally good on Vermont.

Massachusetts

FITCHBURG AREA

FITCHBURG and surrounding towns have one of the largest Finnish populations in the country and, therefore, a group of eager cross-country skiers. Many of them belong to the Finnish Ski Club, which meets in the pine-paneled basement of the colony's Kaleva Home in Fitchburg.

The club, founded in 1946, concentrates on promoting cross-country racing, influenced greatly by its president, Raimo Ahti. Ahti is a 38-year-old bricklayer and mason who is on the U.S. Eastern Cross-Country Ski Team and has been racing in New England since he came to this country over 20 years ago. The club sends many racers, especially young people (there is a Torger Tokle League team), to events all over the region during the winter. The team trains after school in Fitchburg's Saima Park, which has one of the few regularly lighted areas for night cross-country skiing in New England. Saima also is the location of a number of races each season.

The racers in the Finnish club also tour, and Raimo told me that each has his favorite trail in the area's hills. A favorite is the Wapack Trail, maintained by the Appalachian Mountain Club. It extends 21 miles from Ashburnham north across the border into New Hampshire. Two Finnish Ski Club members who have a particular interest in the Wapack Trail are Lenny Amburgey, 28, the bearded director of the Massachusetts Audubon Society's Lincoln Woods Wildlife Sanctuary in Leominister, and Jim Daley, 37, an optical engineer. Lenny and Jim own AD Sports, a new ski touring shop located at Jim's home next to the Wapack on the New Hamp-

Lenny in back of his touring shop. To the left of him, a telescope. In the background, the loyal opposition.

shire border. (The address is Page Hill Road, New Ipswich, N.H.)

They have fashioned one of the best touring centers I have seen: small in operation, but with a good-sized trail system; informal; and offering excellent equipment for sale or rent at reasonable prices.

Jim and Lenny are authoritative when it comes to touring advice. They have toured widely, and both have the racer's knowledge of equipment and technique. Jim, who only took up racing a few years ago, placed 16th in the 1973 Washington's Birthday Race. He brought his training as a marathon runner to the sport. Lenny was once one of the most promising Class A racers until several bouts of illness put him out of serious competition. He still races some, though—with superb technique. His wife, Barbara, 23, who has been racing seriously only a couple of years, finished second in the first Paul Revere Cup at nearby Ft. Devens. She was just behind Martha Rockwell, the best woman racer in the U.S.

Lenny and Jim give lessons, and one of the more interesting deals at their shop is a package comprising a two-hour lesson and complete equipment—skis, boots, bindings, heel plates, poles, wax kit and mounting—all for $75. Another unusual offering is a natural history tour. This is Lenny's specialty.

Lenny and Jim took me on an informal tour of this sort up to Binney Pond over much of the 10 miles of trails they maintain (in addition there's the Wapack). The morning light filtered through birch and mountain laurel, and Lenny pointed out the tracks of a fox and of a raccoon—the path of quills through the snow was easy to recognize. The pond, where the snow was kept dry by the ice, had two big beaver houses on it, one with freshly chewed twigs on the outside.

Jim said they often brought people up to the pond for lunch. We ate raisins and had a drink from a stream by a huge dead chestnut tree. It had been the victim of the disastrous fungus blight early in the century. We skied the circumference of the pond, stopping at one point to smell marsh gas coming up through the snow.

After exploring a few more trails, including a visit to an overlook where Lenny said the Prudential Center in Boston could be seen on a clear day (50 miles away), we headed back to the shop, and Jim's wife served us coffee, tomato soup, warm homemade bread and homemade blueberry pie from berries gathered on their land.

While we were enjoying this sumptuous lunch, several people

came into the shop. They had been scooting around on skis with Alpine parkas on. The temperature was in the 40s by now. They were hot and thirsty.

"Where's the Coke machine?" one of them asked.

We all groaned in unison.

AUDUBON SANCTUARIES

The Massachusetts Audubon Society maintains 44 sanctuaries around the state, with 7000 acres of land whose trails are often suitable for touring. The Society welcomes tourers as much as it welcomes walkers. Besides professionally staffed sanctuaries, there are numerous "open space" areas. The Audubon preserves offer the opportunity to stretch your legs, and observe the environment in an ideal way—without being bothered by snowmobiles, for example.

The Arcadia Sanctuary in Easthampton is a typical area: The largest river marsh in the central Connecticut Valley, these 450 acres are filled with willow and birch and buttonbush. The Sanctuary is an old oxbow of the Connecticut River; it was the site of Indian camps. There is a fine map available.

Another area, the Moose Hill Wildlife Sanctuary in Sharon, south of Boston, presents over 250 acres of woods and meadowland with excellent views from the hills.

The Lincoln Woods in Leominister, where Lenny Amburgey is director, is often used by skiers. If you can catch Lenny you can get good advice on any skiing difficulty.

For information on the sanctuaries and maps, write the Massachusetts Audubon Society headquarters at Lincoln 01773.

WALDEN POND

Those of you who lead lives of quiet or unquiet desperation in the Greater (how much greater?) Boston area should consider a brief

The author paying his extremely humble respects to the ghost of Henry David Thoreau at the site of Thoreau's famous cabin

ski stroll around Walden Pond in Concord as a way to refresh yourselves.

The location of Henry David Thoreau's two years in the woods is now a state reservation. The original character of the pond that I imagined from my readings of *Walden* has been partially preserved. At least in winter it is unprofaned, and there are acres of oak forest around—a physical and spiritual enclave among the suburban tracts.

In the woods there are many trails, including a two-mile one circling the pond, all of which are closed to snowmobiles. There are walkers in the nippy late afternoon. The land was bare of snow the day I visited, so I had to ski on the ice.

Snow does come to Massachusetts. It did in abundance while Thoreau lived at Walden. He tells of plowing through two-foot drifts 8 or 10 miles to keep an appointment with "an old acquaintance among the pines." Skis would have made his trip easier.

Be sure to visit the site of Thoreau's cabin, now commemorated with metal plaques. There aren't many rockpiles honored with august plaques. I think Thoreau would have been amused.

Skiing across the ice—actually on its light coating of snow—I recalled that Thoreau had described the ice as being exceptionally thick, and the pond bottom as unusually deep. Indeed, until he plumbed it, finding it over 100 feet at the greatest depth, the bottom was considered to be unfathomable. In the local lore it was one of those common "bottomless ponds."

But Thoreau observed: "There is a solid bottom everywhere." That's a good sentence to meditate upon as you ski around Walden.

COMMONWEALTH LANDS

In the Boston area, and elsewhere in Massachusetts, there are many state reservations, parks and forests with fine touring. The Miles Standish State Forest in South Carver, 14,000 acres of woods and ponds, has a designated cross-country skiing trail (red triangles) which is a bridle path when there's no snow. It's 14 miles in all its loops, and there are numerous other trails and unplowed roads, although snowmobiles are permitted on many of them.

Other specific cross-country trails may be in the offing, but most preserves are unfortunately ruled by snowmobiles, although the machines are restricted to certain routes. Other possibilities: Bradley Palmer State Park, Hamilton; Hopkinton State Park; Townsend State Forest; Willard Brook State Forest, Townsend; Willowdale State Forest, Ipswich; Chester-Blanford State Forest; Daughters of the American Revolution State Forest in Goshen.

And: Erving State Forest near Greenfield; Granville State Forest; Hawley State Forest; Mohawk Trail State Forest near North Adams; Monroe State Forest; Mount Grace State Forest near Royalston; Robinson State Forest, Agawam; Warwick State Forest in Franklin County; Mount Greylock Reservation near Williamstown; and Savoy Mountain State Forest in Savoy. All these places have marked trails for snowmobiles. At least you'll be on the look-out.

Write to the Division of Forest and Parks, Department of Natural Resources, Commonwealth of Massachusetts, Leverett Saltonstall

The Connecticut River Valley, looking north, from the Wyckoff Park North American Nordic touring center in Holyoke

Building, Government Center, 100 Cambridge St., Boston 02202, for excellent maps of many of the state preserves, complete with trails colored in for the different uses. Many Trustees of Reservations tracts are open to touring, too.

HOLYOKE-NORTHAMPTON AREA

There is a lot of open country here and quite a few steep wooded hills for the more adventurous. Although it is a ski touring tragedy that the huge Quabbin Reservoir is not open to skiers, much land in the sparsely settled region around it is. There are many state lands, some already referred to in this chapter, and Audubon sanctuaries where trails for touring are available.

There are probably more tourers in this region than elsewhere in the state. For one thing the huge UMass-Smith-Amherst-Mount Holyoke-Hampshire student population is taking up touring. Eastern Mountain Sports, between Amherst and Northampton, is a trail information center, as is the North American Nordic shop at the Wyckoff Park golf course off Route 141 in Holyoke. The full range of services is presented, including guided tours to Arcadia Sanctuary and up Mount Tom and Mount Holyoke. The touring center has about five miles of trails in and around the golf course. These are quite scenic. Several of them take you to vantage points where a good portion of the Connecticut Valley is visible. It's an unusual situation to be looking down on factories and housing developments as you skim along.

Indicative of student enthusiasm for touring is the cross-country physical education program at Mount Holyoke College in South Hadley. Upwards of 80 women participated in 1972–73, skiing on the golf course and hockey field and watching their style on video tape.

BERKSHIRES

The Berkshires are being discovered by ski tourers. Ed Bonnivier, who has sold cross-country equipment at his store in Pittsfield for 15 years, is planning to give free lessons in Pittsfield State Forest at 10 a.m. Tuesdays. He also is planning to lay out trails in Springside Park in Pittsfield.

There is the Mount Greylock Reservation, the 15-mile Taconic Ridge Trail (which goes through part of Pittsfield State Forest) and Jiminy Peak downhill area—all places where touring is pursued. Williams College, one of the foremost skiing schools in the country, has a Williams Outing Club Guide, with trails, available for 75 cents (P.O. Box 627, Williamstown). Williams students often ski on Hoosac Mountain near North Adams.

North American Nordic has a center at the Waubeeka Springs Golf Course on Route 7 in South Williamstown. It has a restaurant and 150 acres filled with trails, plus access to many more routes.

OTHER AREAS

Given a good snowstorm, Massachusetts can be as fine a place to ski as Vermont. It is even possible to tour on *Cape Cod,* picking your way through the scrub pine and oak. But you'd better catch it just after the snow falls.

It is possible to ski in Boston. Some people tour along the *Charles River,* and what's wrong with the *Common?* Watch out for muggers. *Fresh Pond Reservoir* in Cambridge, the *Brookline Reservoir* and *Larz Anderson Park* in Brookline are skied. So is the *Chestnut Hill Reservoir* in Newton, but now we're getting into the suburbs, where touring abounds. For example, *Lincoln* has numerous areas. A map is available at the Lincoln Town Hall. There is a route which goes to Walden Pond in Concord. Mike Farney's Lincoln Guide Service on Lincoln Road was organized four years ago. From a modest beginning in his basement, the staff has grown to seven guides. Mike says that "it is more important to me that the skiers appreciate and enjoy the subtle loveliness of winter than learn the discipline of cross-country." Plans are underway to work closely with the Boston Metropolitan District Commission to develop metropolitan ski touring. Overnight trips are sponsored.

There are many organizations within the Boston area that promote ski touring. There are a few Nordic clubs springing up, such as the Scandia Ski Touring Club of Lexington. Formerly all-Alpine clubs are becoming interested in touring. The Boston chapter of the United States Sports Club, formerly the Boston Ski Club, is offering workshops, ski weekends, and beginning touring instruction (325 Harvard St., Brookline 02146).

The Appalachian Mountain Club (5 Joy St., Boston 02108), American Youth Hostels (251 Harvard St., Brookline 02146) and the Sub Sig Outing Club (c/o George Ehrenfried, 102 Aberdeen Ave., Cambridge) sponsor touring activities. And so do the Sierra Club and such private outfits as Eastern Mountain Sports, 1041 Commonwealth Ave., Boston, and Climber's Corner, 49 River St., Cambridge 02139.

Connecticut

LIKE Massachusetts, this is a state that offers superb touring—when there's enough snow. Let us all say a prayer, that the great snow drought be ended. Does anybody know how to do a snow dance?

There are a lot of people in the state who want to tour. For example, last year there were formal touring activities planned for every weekend in the Hartford area. Unfortunately, many had to be cancelled.

The people who planned most of these activities were Judy and Jim Shea of West Hartford (7 Ten Acre Lane 06107), who live at the edge of the 200-acre *West Hartford Reservoir*. These former racers—Jim is U.S. biathalon coach and Judy was a class A racer in college—work tirelessly to promote touring in conjunction with the Ski Touring Council, the Connecticut Ski Council and American Youth Hostels (Hartford Area Council, 315 Pearl Street, Hartford 06103). Biathalon, by the way, is a competition involving skiing and firing a gun at targets.

The Sheas last year put together a calendar of tours, clinics and classes. They had tours every Sunday (weather permitting) at the reservoir, which looks over the Connecticut valley and has rambling hills covered with oak and pine—and only a few miles from downtown Hartford. The reservoir, Judy thinks, is one of the best places to ski in Connecticut. There is a guide to the trails sold in bookstores in the area for $1.

There were also classes given by Judy at the *Buena Vista Golf Course* in West Hartford. Beginners instruction was given by others at the *Carroll Reed Ski Shop* at Drake Hill Mall in Simsbury, at *Great World* in West Simsbury, and at the *Copper Hill Ski Touring Center* in East Granby.

Great World is an outdoors shop specializing in touring. Its owner, Brad Haskell, ran a similar outfit for eight years in Concord, Mass., before moving to West Simsbury a year ago. He is particularly knowledgeable about cross-country skiing, and he and others at the shop lead tours throughout the winter. There are trails right outside the back door. Sometimes classes are held at *McLean Game Refuge* near Simsbury Center. The fee is $5 a person for expert instruction. Last year Haskell ran a Great Race—an open race—complete with the mass start tourers love so well. Haskell has also begun a national "Ski Touring Association" (Box 208, West Simsbury, Conn.), which claims several hundred members. It has a newsletter and has started a system of recognition for distances toured.

Another major center of touring last year was the Copper Hill facility, one of the North American Nordic chain. As I write this, the future of Copper Hill as a touring center is up in the air, but undoubtedly the North American Nordic people will have a place in Connecticut. Last year Copper Hill offered great touring when there was snow. There are 14 miles of trails, one past a Revolutionary era copper mine, another passing by the ancient Newgate Prison, one of the more fascinating historical sites in New England.

Farther to the west, in Norfolk, the *Blackberry River Inn* last season opened a touring program with a certified instructor. There are 10 miles of groomed trails through the Berkshire Hills and a rental and sales operation. Farther south, *Woodbury Ski and Racquet* on Route 47 maintains some trails and has rentals and instruction.

All over Connecticut there are excellent opportunities to ski in the state parks and forests. Last year the best skiing in the state was to be had in *Tunxis State Forest* near the Massachusetts border in Hartland—fine unplowed roads. The State Department of Environmental Protection has an informational sheet for ski tourers on where to ski. Among the recommended areas are *John A. Minetto* and *Sunnybrook State Park* in Torrington (many meadows), *Osbornedale State Park* in Derby (trails and meadows), *Wadsworth*

Falls State Park in Middlefield (wooded and open trails), and *Natchaug State Forest* in Eastford (forest roads).

Powder Ridge in Middlefield has taken the lead in promoting touring among the downhill areas. Instruction and rentals and sales are available. The state-marked *Mattabassett Trail* runs from north to south right across the top of the mountain. *Mount Southington* has a sizable tract laced with trails. The area has no formal cross-country program, but the people there told me that if the demand warranted it they would institute one.

White's Woods in Litchfield has lots of woods roads and level terrain. There is a map available from the White Memorial Foundation. The Litchfield Hills Ski Shop (S. Lake Street and Route 25) has equipment.

Up in the northwestern corner of the state there is usually pretty good snowfall and a good number of ski tourers, particularly in the *Salisbury* area. A road which soon becomes unplowed heads north from the Town Hall in the direction of *Mount Riga*, the highest point in Connecticut. The Mount Riga plateau is often skied by Salisbury skiers. Nine miles south of Salisbury, in *Sharon*, there is a 500-acre Audubon sanctuary which welcomes tourers.

There are so many "civilized" woods in Connecticut—full of unplowed roads and well-trodden paths—that touring trails, as well as open land, are not hard to come by. People in the Greenwich-Stamford area can use their numerous golf courses.

The Connecticut Walk Book, listed in the Appendix, contains hundreds of trails.

Rhode Island

A FELLOW saw me starting to write this chapter and chuckled: "Gee. It's nice you're doing something for poor little Rhode Island."

Rhode Islanders always have to put up with such condescensions! Although I used to live here, I've never toured in Rhode Island, but it's full of great ski touring terrain. The only problem is snow. Since the touring boom began a couple of years ago, most Rhode Islanders have had to drive north to get in much touring.

The state Department of Natural Resources is thinking about the needs of tourers. Official ski touring trails are in the cards, but there are plenty of trails to tour on right now. First off, try the northwestern part of the state. The *George Washington Management Area* and *Casimir Pulaski State Park* have a good number of footpaths and gravel roads—built by the Civilian Conservation Corps in the 1930s. This area, which gets more snowfall than the rest of the state, is also quite heavily used by snowmobiles. Two specific trail possibilities are the Walkabout Trail and the Peck Pond Spur Trail. There is an Appalachian Mountain Club map of this area.

Farther south, there is an A.M.C. trail system—with map—in the *Arcadia Management Area, Beach Pond State Park* and *Dawley Memorial State Forest.* Route 165 provides a number of access points. However, as you get closer to the warm waters of Narragansett Bay and Block Island Sound, snowfall often has a finale of rain.

I remember sleigh riding in the moonlight in *Goddard Memorial State Park* on Greenwich Bay. There are certainly opportunities for skiing in that park as well as in other parks in built-up areas close to the water, such as *Lincoln Woods State Park, Colt State Park* and *Roger Williams Park* in Providence. Again, don't forget golf courses.

The downhill ski areas might provide limited territory for touring: *Ski Valley,* Cumberland; *Diamond Hill,* Cumberland; *Yawgoo Valley,* Exeter; and *Pine Top,* Escoheag (West Greenwich).

One shop in the state has a great interest in cross-country skiing: The Summit Shop, 185 Wayland Avenue, Providence 02906. They give clinics, show movies and carry Bonna, Toppen, Trak and Alfa brands. Several people from the shop are racers, and last winter three engaged in the grueling Canadian Marathon. They skied a total—all three combined—of 180 miles in 15 hours. Competing against 1200 others, they told me they brought back a silver and two bronze medals.

I doubt if there is a Nordic club as such, but the Narragansett Bay Wheelmen, a group of nearly 200 cyclists, plan to tour in the winter. The president is Warren Hinterland, 187 Garden St., Cranston.

Cooking in the snow can be amazingly easy if you don't have to build a fire. A Bleuet butane stove is being used to cook—in a matter of a few minutes—a one-pot meal. The pot cover is a near-must in the winter.

Lunch on the Trail

ONE OF the most delightful things about ski touring is the opportunity for winter picnics. The domain of winter nourishment can be almost limitless, especially for day trips. If you're willing to pack it, you can take almost anything with you: fresh bread, fruit, meat ranging from filet mignon to live lobster. Spoilage is rarely a consideration on a winter day trip, and things generally don't freeze next to your back. Some people don't even mind carrying a picnic table if it's only a mile or two.

Usually, though, there are limitations involved in lunch on the snowy trail. The important thing to remember is to take whatever appeals to you—like a case of champagne—but there nevertheless exists advice that will make things easier.

FIRE

In the Emergency Winter Camp chapter I will describe how to start a fire in the winter woods. When it's not an emergency, it's much easier to do, but it is still not easy. A few suggestions: Carry some tinder in a plastic bag. Make sure *before* you light the fire you're going to have enough wood on hand. Don't throw gasoline onto a fire already started; sprinkle your twigs, etc., with it beforehand; there are commercial fire starters and primers. Strike matches into the wind, cupping the head of the match into the palm of your hand, letting the flame burn up the matchstick. Make sure your pyramid of twigs has plenty of space for oxygen. Don't overload the fire with too many big pieces too fast. Being a good fire builder essentially means not smothering the fire. The best places for fires are usually in fireplaces at specified campsites, even in the winter. Just clean the snow out. A good lunch spot is out of the wind, near water, and in the sun—not an easy order. Position stones so you can set pots on them. There are small grills that can fit into the smallest packs.

But do you really need a fire? If it's real cold a fire will provide some warmth, but not much, and it often is so much trouble in wintertime that the time spent standing around shivering in sweaty clothes may not be worth it. A stove, however, is easy to operate and much quicker. A growing number of people don't like to have fires in the woods and are concerned with leaving the environment as untouched as possible in their passage through it. I no longer take an axe in the woods. You can generally get what you want with your hands.

There are a great many tiny stoves on the market. They burn gasoline, kerosene, propane, butane, alcohol and naphtha. Svea is very popular, weighing a pound and a half, fueled by white gas. But from observing the antics of my friends trying to get one lighted I am content with my untemperamental butane Bleuet stove with expendable cartridges. The only problem is at very low temperatures it is not supposed to work. But I generally only cook in the unsheltered outdoors when it's no lower than the 20s, and it seems to work fine then.

WATER

You can bring it along, dip it out of a stream or spring, or melt snow. Water is heavy, thus the argument against packing it. Winter mountain streams are usually safe, but you can be sure if you treat water with purification tablets. Melting snow is a tedious process. It takes a lot of snow to get a little water. If you can, put some water in the bottom of the pot before you press the snow down into it. Or make sure all the bottom surface of the pot is covered with snow. Melt to liquid before adding more snow. These precautions prevent scorching. If you fill a canteen with snow and preferably a little water, the snow may have sloshed into water in a few hours. Clean snow is quite sterile. The twigs and needles in it can be skimmed off or will drop to the bottom.

UTENSILS

Keep pots and other gear to an absolute minimum. They will take up a lot of space in your small day pack. Most people don't like to ski with big packs, even for an afternoon hike, so I'm assuming lightness and little bulk are important. One-pot meals are common because they make cooking and cleaning easier. Big juice cans with wire handles can replace pots. They are disposable and can be flattened for storage. A pot cover makes cooking immensely quicker. The whole idea in winter outdoors cookery is to get something to eat *fast* before you get too cold from inaction.

For individual servings, nothing beats a Sierra Club cup. Otherwise: a deep plastic plate and a plastic cup. (Plastic holds the heat in.) Add a small knife-spoon-fork combination, or maybe you'll want a spoon, using your pocket combination knife when you have to slice a hunk of cheese. The cook might want to take along a large spoon. If you're traveling with a group, everyone doesn't have to carry a stove and a pot. It's more efficient to pool resources, plan your menu and appoint a cook before you start out.

Disposable plates and cups may make for a light pack on the way back (you can burn them if you have a fire), but they have a way of becoming litter.

LIGHTNESS, SMALL BULK

Water is what generally makes food heavy, so dehydrated food is often used by those who have to back pack. Freeze-dried food is now widely available in camping and mountain sports stores and in some ski shops. It ranges from steak to chicken stew. It is light, nonbulky, and amazingly easy to prepare. The major disadvantage is cost. As an alternative you can outfit yourself quite completely at a good supermarket. Groceries can be rendered less heavy and, especially, bulky if you remove the food from the containers and put it into tightly sealed plastic bags. Plastic bottles are available for cooking oil, honey, etc. Unbreakability in a pack is a big plus, too.

SIMPLICITY

Cooking is made much easier if you combine things *before* you strike off, such as dry ingredients for a soup, pancakes and so forth. Soups are popular in winter camps because boiling and simmering are simple. Broiling by putting food on sticks and twirling it in the fire is as easy as frying. You can get covered skillets useful for boiling and frying. However, things that are fried or broiled in the winter tend to lose their heat fast—soups stay hot awhile.

Heating dishwater is unnecessary. For the time being wipe off pots with snow, using a few paper towels which you can burn. Or simply pack an old rag which can double as a potholder. Some people use their pocket bandanna for all this!

The ultimate in lunchtime simplicity is not bothering to stop at all to eat, but to munch away all during the day. The old standbys —sausage, cheese, chocolate bars, dried apricots, raisins—can seem mouth-wateringly delicious when eaten at several beautiful spots along the way. There's always sandwiches.

"Gorp" was created for people who don't believe in stopping for an official meal. This is just a plastic bag full of candies, crackers, pieces of meat, dried fruit, cheese cubes, nuts, whatever your palate desires all thrown in together. Eat gorp in handfuls whenever hunger strikes. Incidentally, when you're doing some long hard touring, it is easier for the body to digest several snacks during the day than one large meal.

It's a good idea, in any case, to have plenty of tidbits along, especially sugary, high-energy foods. Raisins and chocolates are traditional, but they take quite some time to be digested. If you want a really quick lift, take dextrose pills. These work in a matter of minutes. Also, there are several high-energy powders which can be mixed in water. Lemonade or grape juice powders mixed in your canteen water provide a tasty way of getting lots of sugar and vitamin C. You could, of course, fill a thermos with *hot* drink. If you are skiing on a bitter cold day, filling your canteen with hot water in the morning will ensure that you won't be drinking an ice and water mix later on. You can eat snow. Hold it in your mouth to let it melt before you swallow it. Pour fruit-flavored syrup on some snow in a cup and you have sherbet.

Take a little more than you think you need to ward off the Galloping Munchies—fairly common on the touring trail. Also, it's always nice to have extra for hungry natives or an emergency such as a blizzard that requires you to camp out.

NUTRITION

Beside sugar for quick lifts, on a day's hike you don't have to think much about specific nutritional needs. Be sure, however, to eat a good breakfast. You'll be mainly running on the steam provided by it. Carbohydrates are the mainstays of energy production, so lots of breakfast toast, pancakes, home-fried potatoes and fruit would be a good idea. Unless you're in a race you probably won't need salt tablets, but presalting your food is a good idea. Salt lost through heavy sweating can lead to exhaustion.

SHOPPING LIST

The following groceries should be considered as possible trail foods. They are cheap, easy to use, light and won't spoil.

· Fruit: dried raisins, prunes, apricots, dates.
· Nuts.
· Soybeans, roasted.
· Seeds: sunflower, sesame.
· Cheeses: Monterey jack, cheddar, Swiss, gouda.
· Meats: beef jerky, dry salami and sausage, Canadian bacon, dried fish, canned tuna, canned chicken.
· Eggs: powdered, scrambled egg mixes.
· Breads: crackers, flatbreads, pumpernickel, French bread.
· Cereals: oatmeal, grits, cornmeal, wheat germ, Familia (cereal, nuts, fruit), other dry cereals.
· Starches: Spaghetti, noodles, macaroni, rice, instant rice and noodle dinners, instant potatoes.

· Vegetables: vegetable flakes, popcorn.
· Soups, dried: onion, pea, chicken noodle, beef noodle.
· Cooking oil.
· Oleomargarine.
· Sweets: honey, molasses, sugar, chocolate, candies, cookies.
· Seasonings.
· Beverages: Instant Breakfast, instant milk, Tang, tea, instant coffee, lemonade, grapeade, cocoa, carob powder, bouillon cubes.

PUTTING IT TOGETHER

This is the whole idea: mixing things. Make a hefty soup or a casserole. A late-morning trail breakfast can be a pot of hot cereal —oatmeal, say—fortified with dried fruit and bits of meat. Stir dried milk into the cereal water. Add wheat germ for an excellent source of protein. Wheat germ can be eaten by itself as a cereal. If you don't like it uncooked, you can toast it beforehand. (Toasting wheat germ at home is cheaper than buying toasted wheat germ in the stores.)

Some gorps make good trail breakfasts. Mix dried fruit, nuts, seeds, toasted wheat germ, toasted oatmeal, shredded coconut, etc., and eat with cold or warm milk.

How about putting together an omelette? With cheese, meat and seasoning?

Or take the cheese and make a fondue with a pot of soup accompanying.

Or maybe have a cup of bouillon followed by a pot of stew. Stew can be started with water, fat or oil, some dry soup mix or sauce mix, and seasonings. Then add some roasted soybeans, if you like, and meat or fish. Add vegetable flakes, seeds, instant potatoes for thickening, and wheat germ.

There are all sorts of concoctions possible with rice. Add a dry soup mix to the boiling water before adding the rice. Pour in some fat and the seasonings, roasted soybeans, meat, seeds, vegetable flakes, and dried fruit. Whatever you like. Experiment. After this

Jim Daley fills a plastic canteen with icy water from a clean mountain stream. You cool off fast drinking this.

has cooked a few minutes, add the rice. Create wholly different concoctions by using noodles instead of rice, and vary seasonings.

There are an incredible number of one-pot dishes you can make on the trail. Dig out your cookbooks and see what can be transferred to the outdoors.

Don't forget some good hearty wine. Wine bags don't break, and are lighter than bottles. Wine tastes better out of a bag than a plastic canteen.

Training

GENERALITIES

WHAT is necessary to get people to exercise more is a whole new state of mind. A state of mind which assumes that running and walking and bicycling are normal activities. The reason people in many other countries are in so much better shape than we (it's a fact) is because they walk, cycle and otherwise exercise in the normal course of daily life. It is not because they are more virtuous than we. As they get automobiles, ski lifts and snowmobiles, they degenerate in physical condition, too.

I think getting people to exercise more can only be accomplished by a very radical change in our way of approaching the world— not as something to exploit, but to be replenished; not as something to conquer, but to respect; not as something whose demands are to be circumvented, but whose demands are to be honored. I am not at all sure this will be done.

But recently the environmental movement has articulated in words and deeds an approach to life quite distinct from the prevailing one. If this attitude is more than a fad, more than a romantic reaction, then maybe it will be possible to fashion a postindustrial civilization where machines would be rationally used.

On the individual level, this would mean people would exercise more—naturally. Now, as individuals, we can change our thinking to create our own private postindustrial state—and we will find ourselves exercising more. So, before I offer specific ways to improve your body through exercise, let me emphasize that the most important way to accomplish this goal is to change your way of thinking. You need to rethink the bases of your life.

SPECIFICS

For the purpose of physical training, ski touring is primarily an endurance activity—or as they call it nowadays, an "aerobic" activity. Touring forces the body to demand more oxygen, and, in doing so, strengthens the heart, the respiratory muscles, blood vessels and general muscle tone, and increases the oxygen-carrying capacity of the blood. Resistance to heart disease and the ability to recover from it are therefore increased.

The sports that are the best training for cross-country skiing are other endurance activities such as walking, jogging, running, swimming, cycling and rowing. (Rowing on the Charles would be the ultimate in status in training for cross-country skiing in New England.) Do these consistently throughout the year and you will be in good shape for ski touring.

There are other sports which, depending on how conscientiously you play them, can be endurance activities. Examples would be tennis, badminton, volleyball, and even golf (with vigorous walking). Squash and handball are quite active sports. All these are less monotonous than running, and they offer the elements of competition and development of elaborate skills.

Indoor "exercises" at home are probably the most difficult for most people to do because they are boring. They can, however, be quite good preparation for cross-country. Concentrate on wind activities such as running in place. Muscle exercises are good supplements. If you run in the off season you may not keep your arms and upper body in the shape required for an easy transition to hard and fast cross-country skiing. And calisthenics—particularly push-ups and sit-ups—are excellent warm-up activities for your aerobic activity, be it running or ski touring.

A good warm-up is stretching the muscles (toe touching, back bends, etc.). This is the first thing you should do; then proceed to calisthenics, followed by running or skiing. You can warm up simply by running or skiing slowly at first, then building up speed. Warming up is necessary to prevent muscle and joint difficulties.

Cooling down is just as important—perhaps more so. If you go from a hot and heavy workout quickly to a state of complete inaction, the reasons are complicated but it taxes the heart. And going from vigorous exercise directly to a hot shower, an overheated room or a sauna is worse. Cool off first by walking around a bit.

For your body to benefit from ski touring, you need to ski regularly—more than once a week. Above all, don't try to ski 15 miles the first time out if you haven't been exercising. You'll have sore muscles, and if you're an older person you might bring on much more serious problems. The nice thing about touring is that it can be as hard as you make it. You can go as far and speedily as you wish, over terrain of your own choosing. It can be only a pleasant little walk. On the other hand, if you are truly interested in exercise, then you have to really exercise. Push yourself a little, if you've built up to it. It actually can be fun. Besides increasing your aerobic capacity, touring will give you stronger muscles—arms, too, unlike running—and improve your agility.

Strong exercise when it's quite cold out will generally be harmless. When it's extremely cold and you're constantly skiing into a stiff wind, then it is possible to strain your heart. This is particularly true if you run yourself to exhaustion and are not very fit. A scarf over the face will warm the air before you suck it in and also help prevent frostbite.

Try warming up before you go outside, since cold tends to stiffen the muscles.

Emergency Winter Camp, Getting Unlost & First Aid

EMERGENCY CAMP

THIS is not a book about winter camping. Nevertheless, it is good to know what should be done if a day tourer finds himself forced unexpectedly to spend a night out in the woods.

This should be an extremely rare occurrence in New England. It is almost always better to keep skiing after dark if you can follow the trail and if you have hope of reaching civilization soon. In most of New England help is seldom very far away. Even if a member of your party has fallen into a stream, it is usually safer to high-tail-it to the nearest road than to stop, try to build a fire and dry him out. If he's wearing wool and works hard at skiing, he'll usually keep warm enough, though he may become somewhat encrusted with ice, which will insulate him anyway. Incidentally, if you roll in the snow after a dunking, the snow mops up a lot of water.

You might be forced to bivouac if you are quite lost. Generally, if you can see at all, follow a fence line, streams downhill, your tracks back, or pick the most reasonable compass course and follow it, you're usually better off to keep going after dark. You might not reach your destination right away, but you'll get there eventually.

There may be a time, however, when you're lost after dark in a heavy snowfall and you know you're miles from other people. You decide to camp out. It would be especially wise to camp out before you become dangerously exhausted.

How should you bivouac? First of all, you're not in much trouble if you have a good (dry) down sleeping bag or even a good down parka packed away. Dig a trench in the snow in some sheltered spot. Make it a foot or two deep and a bit longer and wider than your body. Use your skis or extra ski tip to dig with. A good place to clear out a trench is around evergreens where there may be some space between the trunk and the lowest branches. Here, you may have to do practically no digging. Don't get sweaty. You may want to take your parka off while digging. Line the bottom of the trench with branches from a fir or spruce. Never lie directly on snow. Line the sides of the trench with branches. Spread out your sleeping bag, arrange your skis parallel above your trench, and pull lots of boughs over the skis across the top of the trench. Falling snow will collect on top of the skis and insulate you further. If you have only a parka, put your feet (keep your boots on) in your pack. Loosen the boots. Eat whatever you've got left over from lunch. Pleasant dreams.

Your trench will not drop in temperature much below 32 degrees. If there are two of you, build a slightly larger trench and snuggle up. If you have to, both get into one sleeping bag and if you have another one, fit that bag over it. No one will ever know. Some people suggest snow caves, but you have to have just the right kind of drift for it, and it takes longer to build.

Unless you're not very cold or tired a fire in such situations is a luxury (except when you have a portable stove) because it usually consumes so much time and energy that it isn't worthwhile building. But if you don't have a sleeping bag, it may be necessary to keep from freezing. It's also a necessity if you are wet. Building a fire in daylight is infinitely easier than after nightfall, but I doubt if most people will realize the extent of their predicament until darkness.

Find a sheltered spot, in the lee of some boulders perhaps. You probably won't find any dead wood lying around, but you should be able to find some on the lower parts of trees. Get all sizes, starting with the smallest twigs you can find. Scoop out a depression in the snow, put some relatively flat pieces of wood, or a rock, in the

SKI – TOURING RULES

1. DON'T SKI ALONE!
2. IN CASE OF ACCIDENT, KEEP INJURED PERSON WARM, & RETURN FOR HELP.
3. CARRY A MAP & SPARE TIP.
4. LISTEN TO PEOPLE WITH EXPERIENCE.

Trapp Lodge rules. But at some point you should ski alone.

bottom of it, and build your fire there. For tinder, use rolled-up tiny strips of a candy bar wrapper, or birch bark. Add progressively bigger pieces of wood in a pyramid. The paraffin in your wax kit makes a good fire primer. Keep a supply of wood handy and stay up all night keeping the fire going. Position yourself between it and the rocks to take advantage of the oven effect. Build several fires and get in the middle of them. Have happy thoughts. Remember those old songs you used to sing around the campfire.

If you don't have matches or a sleeping bag or big parka, you are in trouble. I hate to dash Boy Scout hopes, but your chances of starting a fire without matches are pretty slim. My recommendation is to keep moving. Head downhill. Stay calm. Don't exhaust yourself, however. Chances are that when you're so exhausted you want to fall asleep—actually it's more like falling unconscious—you will never wake up. At least keep hopping around in one place.

SURVIVAL GEAR

Whenever I go into real wilderness, even on a day trip, I like to take a sleeping bag and a portable stove, great for fixing a hot lunch. Even when the country isn't so wild I like to have the following survival gear in my day pack:

· Matches in a waterproof container.
· Candle.
· Whistle.
· Extra food: candy, nuts, raisins, etc. Wrappers can be used for tinder.

- Mirror (for signaling).
- Knife.
- Map.
- Compass.
- Flashlight or headlamp.
- Extra batteries, extra bulb.
- Space blanket. One of these, the ultimate in insulation, might in a jam take the place of sleeping bag or fire. They are inexpensive, come folded in hand-sized packages, but unfold big enough to wrap yourself in. Frankly, I've never had to use one, but they may be quite effective in a snow trench, or simply as you huddle among some rocks, especially if you can wrap it around you, open in front, as you sit before a fire.
- First aid kit (see below).

See also the chapters on equipment and clothing.

GETTING UNLOST

If you have a map and compass, try to use them to follow a route out. If you have a map and can ski or walk, you're probably not in danger. If you don't have either a map or compass, pick a landmark and walk towards it, then another one, telling your general direction by the sun. The stream-and fence-following methods you attempted the night before are more easily accomplished in the daylight. If you come to a place where there's lots of dead wood, like a bog around a frozen lake, and you know people will be looking for you, build a big fire and pile green boughs that will smoke. That would be a good place to spend the next night, keeping the fire blazing.

The way to avoid getting lost is usually:

1. Have a map and compass.
2. Going with someone who knows the area.

The way to get people to go after you is:

1. Telling somebody, like a ranger or the farmer in whose yard you park your car, where you're going and when you're coming back.

2. Leaving a note telling route and return time under a windshield wiper of your car. Number 1 is to be preferred, but do both.

Know what the weather forecast is, and plan your trip accordingly. Don't overestimate your strength.

FIRST AID

It would be a good idea for people who tour a great deal to take a Red Cross first aid course or at least read a good text on the subject. Let's look at the two main winter disasters: frostbite and hypothermia.

FROSTBITE

Frostbite is common among downhill skiers. They face high winds and often are relatively inactive—while on ski lifts, for example. It is less common among tourers, but still is a danger. The way to prevent it is keep the whole body warm, keep out of the wind as much as possible, avoid tight clothing on the hands and feet, don't touch metal objects with bare hands when it's extremely cold, keep the feet and hands always dressed warmly (face masks or balaclavas are useful), and don't get exhausted—which also means don't skip meals. By the way, frostbite frequently afflicts the intoxicated.

Frostbite, which may be thought of as "frozen" tissue, usually hits the face, hands or feet—the extremities. It appears as a hard, waxy, white area on the skin. Skiers should occasionally check each others' noses, ears, chins, etc. in high winds, especially. Numbness with a tingling sensation as the skin is rewarmed does not mean frostbite. No more feeling of cold at a particular part may. If you freeze a foot, it will seem as hard as a rock. Don't let feet and hands go numb and stay numb for a long time.

Treatment for serious frostbite should be undertaken by a physician. If this is impossible, the afflicted part should be stripped and thawed out in water heated to a temperature between 108 and 112 degrees for 20 minutes. A very rough way of approximating this if you don't have a thermometer is that the water should feel hot but shouldn't burn. In addition, keep the patient's body warm. Make him drink hot beverages. Do not put a frozen part next to a fire. Once a foot has been thawed out, don't walk on it. In fact, do not rub or disturb a thawed part in any way. You can severely damage it. Carry the patient out to civilization on a litter. He is very liable to infection and needs medical care. Because a severely frostbitten part becomes inoperable when rewarmed, it often is better to let a person walk on his frozen feet out to civilization rather than do a poor job thawing him out. Slow thawing can be quite damaging—so is too much heat.

For minor frostbite, pressing a warm hand on a nose, putting fingers in a warm armpit, or even putting toes against someone's warm stomach—sheltering the whole operation—all work quite well. Don't rub the affected part, ever. Press it firmly.

HYPOTHERMIA

Hypothermia is also known as "exposure." It also is known as freezing to death. Simply put, it is the lowering of the temperature of the body's core. Lower your body temperature more than 10 degrees and you're facing death. Hypothermia can be prevented by wearing plenty of clothing, keeping dry, and not becoming exhausted. Hypothermia often is a complication of shock arising from injury. Symptoms are shivering, paleness, fast pulse, slurred speech, mental confusion, stumbling, drowsiness. Eventually the hypothermic patient will become unconscious and the pulse will be slow and irregular.

Treatment is rewarming. Do something fast. Someone should climb into a sleeping bag with the patient, and put that bag into another sleeping bag. Putting him in a sleeping bag alone is not enough as his body is not producing enough heat. The patient should be fed hot drinks if he's still conscious. Get that core warmed! If he's unconscious, consider a hot enema. Be ready to apply artificial respiration and external heart massage. If he recovers, get him to a hospital.

You can suffer from hypothermia when the temperature is well above freezing. All you need is the right combination of inadequate clothing and exhaustion, with wetness frequently a factor. Skinny men are particularly susceptible.

FIRST AID KIT

Those getting into serious mountaineering should consult first aid texts and seek medical advice when putting together a really complete first aid kit. These people should probably be equipped with, and know how to use, various drugs—pain killers and antibiotics, for example. Make sure you have prescriptions. I don't want to read about the first ski tourer who got busted.

The following is a suggested kit for day tours and overnights:
- Bandaids, several sizes.
- Roll of gauze and gauze pads.
- Adhesive tape.
- Scissors (for cutting gauze, tape, clothing).
- Ace elastic bandage.
- Safety pins.
- Dial soap.
- Moleskin (for blisters and blister prevention).
- Aspirin.
- Salt tablets.
- First aid cream.
- Water purification tablets.

Racing: Portrait of Bob Gray

BOB GRAY, at 34 the oldest member of the U.S. Ski Team, is finally the nation's top cross-country ski racer. It is fitting that the Nordic fates have allowed Bob to have his schuss in the sun. He has worked for it longer than any American racer, bearing the burden of all our cross-country competitors. Which is to accustom themselves to finishing generally no higher than 20th in the big international contests.

This past winter—his best ever—his travail culminated in a triple victory at the national championships in Minneapolis. He was first in the 30-kilometer, first in the 50-kilometer, and a member of the winning men's relay team. His 50-kilometer trophy was taken away from him, however, as a result of a minor technicality. The rules required that a racer finish with at least one of the skis he started out with. But the assistant who waxed one of Bob's skis after every lap inadvertently gave him the wrong ski on the last lap, so Bob was disqualified—in this, his specialty. He was sad but not sore.

His victories come just in time. For time is catching up with him. This winter will probably be his last season.

"Everybody else is giving up," he says in explanation. "All the guys I skied with for years—Mike Gallagher and Mike Elliott—have gone."

To some degree Bob's preeminence depends upon the departure of these two from the racing scene—both into helping sell touring gear. Gray, Gallagher and Elliott were the Big Three of cross-country racing for years, but Gallagher and Elliott, to speak only of Americans, gave Bob number two or three place in many races.

Bob Gray, right, and U.S. Cross-Country Coach Marty Hall before the start of the 1973 Paul Revere Cup Race

(Although Bob raced against and beat Gallagher in the Minneapolis championships).

Bob hung in there, perhaps to get the recognition he may have felt he deserved after his long years—20 of racing—in devotion to a little-celebrated sport.

Now, however, Bob Gray feels the same call as Gallagher and Elliott—to get into the world and start working on a lasting career.

"But I'll stay independent," he says. He referred to all the racers who have thrown their lot in with the big corporations that are trying to take advantage of the burgeoning touring market.

Bob's lot is the West Hill Ski Shop in Putney, Vt., two years in existence, and, planned for this season, the West Hill Touring Center. He hopes to have 30 miles of maintained trails and many more old logging roads available in the hills above the shop. The shop and the center represent the incarnation of a dream for Bob—to take advantage of all those racing years and make a living from them.

The nexus of trails he is working on will center at his new home on the top of Putney Mountain. It is one of two houses on the summit of a 17-mile ridge. The original part of the house was a camp bought by his father 30 years ago. His parents still live in Putney, Bob's home town. Bob went to the Putney School, where his father worked as a maintenance man and his mother as a housekeeper, and Bob skied there under the tuteledge of John Caldwell. Until a couple of years ago, Bob worked for the school as athletic director and head of the student work program.

I visited Bob on a bright sunny day in the middle of April. There was still plenty of snow on top of the mountain, but it was melting. The steep three-mile dirt road up was a stream. Bob said he ran up it every day as his gesture toward conditioning during this season. His wife Sue and their two young children were away.

The ample rambling house was made of wood and lots of glass; old barn boards covered the inside walls. It was filled with books, plants soaking up the sun and Audubon prints on the walls. A frisky dog bounced around. Boards and a sander and other machinery lay about. He still had much to do on the house, he said. He had been working on it four years. We sat at a big old wooden table beneath an antique chandelier and looked out upon what must be one of the most impressive views in Vermont. Out over the birch and maples 60 miles of New Hampshire and Massachusetts stretched away to the southeast. A hazy blue Mount Monadnock dominating the horizon. Bob sliced bread from a loaf he had just baked and served it with butter, coffee in earthenware mugs, and a jar of rhubarb.

Bob looks athletic: His muscular leanness left not an atom of fat anywhere; his taut boyish face—with its shock of brown hair and square jaw—makes him look 25. He wore old trousers and a blue, wrinkled work shirt. He spoke fast, assertively.

"A while ago I thought touring would overtake Alpine skiing in ten years," he said. "I think now it might within five—in numbers of people doing it." He foresaw no end to the boom nor to commercialization. "It bothers me. There must be a ceiling on prices somewhere. A few years ago John (Caldwell) was importing directly and selling skis for $20 a pair. Now I have to pay $46 *wholesale* for the same kind of ski."

One of the ways out of the equipment cost spiral, he suggested, would be for the U.S. to avoid importing skis and make its own instead. "We wouldn't have to import hickory," he said. "With the dollar devaluation and the standard of living always going up in Scandinavia, and the taxes going up there too, things are just going to get much more expensive."

Gray, of course, is in commerce himself, and in the next breath he told of how it hasn't been all that easy to make money from cross-country skiing. "The first year was good," he said, "but this year wasn't. I was gone all winter racing, and I couldn't push things. You have to do that, you know. I'm trying to think of ways to advertize."

I suggested the meager snowfall might have had something to do with it.

"Well, if there isn't snow where the people are—in Massachusetts and Connecticut, say—maybe that discourages them, but it's been pretty good skiing all season here. That's something you should put in your book, by the way. Most people have a completely wrong idea about what makes for good skiing. They think unless there's a lot of fresh powder you shouldn't bother to go, but lots of fresh powder isn't good, and New England really has the best skiing in the U.S. and I've skied everywhere.

"If you don't have enough snow where you are, there will always be snow up in the hills. Look around here at all the snow in the middle of April. And there is nothing better than the January thaw. It settles it. Even a rainstorm is good. Three feet of snow will settle to two-and-a-half base, then there will be three inches of new snow —perfect. The only thing we've got against us is the ice."

The subject of snow got us into equipment. Bob is cautious about non-wax skis. "They work fairly well under ideal conditions," he said, adding that he prefers fish-scale to mohair because "You can wax it a little." But his preference is for wooden, waxable skis, although he said he felt the Fischer ski "is where it's going." These are lightweight, virtually unbreakable metal skis with plastic bottoms which hold wax almost as well as wood.

Bob believes, as do most racers, that recreational cross-country skiers should not be forced into heavy skis and boots and cable bindings out of what he would term an exaggerated notion of being secure. He pushes lightweight gear—pin bindings, for example. "Comfort is important, and I think what really excites people—it's what excites me—is the feeling of *movement*."

"Movement" naturally brought us to technique. "Touring is the same thing as racing," he said. "It's just a matter of progression. You use the same rhythm; you just build it up."

I asked him about American racing technique. He laughed. "Our technique is okay, we just don't know how fast you can go. I would win at the Squaw Valley Olympics if I could go as fast as I do right now," he said. "People are just going faster and faster, that's the thing—not any big change in technique."

Bob was not at Squaw Valley in 1960, but he was at Grenoble in 1968 and Sapporo in '72. And he has been on three F.I.S. (Fédération Internationale du Ski) teams: '62, '66, and '70. He made his first F.I.S. team while finishing up at the University of Colorado, where his coach was Bob Beattie, who went on to become head U.S. Ski Team coach. Bob went to Colorado because of Beattie, whom he describes as "over-eager but fantastic."

The biggest influence on his skiing, however, was John Caldwell, first while Bob was a student at Putney, then while Caldwell was U.S. Head Cross-Country Coach. "He's been kind of a guiding light," Gray said.

I asked Bob about what we might expect in the way of racers from the Putney School in years hence. "Well, skiing now is not so big there as it used to be," he said. "I guess the type of student has changed. They're not so competitive now."

But there is Bill Koch, who's only 17 and whom Gray compares to Tim Caldwell, 19, a recent Putney graduate who's attending Dartmouth as did his father. Both Koch and Caldwell are members of the U.S. Team.

"If we had a hundred Billy Kochs and Tim Caldwells, we might win some medals," Bob remarked. "Both have been training now for six or seven years. Either one could win a medal sometime."

Bob Gray has never won a medal. The best he has done in an FIS or Olympic race was 22nd in the 50-kilometer F.I.S. competition in 1970. An American, in fact, has never won a cross-country F.I.S. or Olympic medal. But in "world caliber competition" Bob has placed 8th in a 15-kilometer race and 12th in a 50-kilometer, his specialty. Perhaps his best race, however, and the one he seemed to take the most pride in describing was the 1970 Vasaloppet, when he placed 27th out of a field of 9000. "Caldwell told me that the Vasa was terrible, that I'd be stuck in crowds and would just have to shuffle along. But I started in the first row and was free all the way." He started in the first row because of his international racing status.

What would it take for the U.S. to produce racers who win medals? Bob answered by launching into a discussion of what's wrong with the U.S. Team's race preparations.

"Our training is one thing. We train too hard. We peak too early in the season. I think in '72 we might have cleaned up in the Olympics if we hadn't peaked about a week before. We had just gone too hot and heavy early in the season.

"We need to have a better progression for training. I mean, if you're running 20 miles a day in August, what will you be doing in January?

"It's interesting to see what the Norwegians do, because they're the best in the world. During the summer they'll do some easy track two or three days a week while holding down a full-time job. Their first training camp isn't until September. In summer they'll also do some roller skating [special ski-like roller skates] and some easy, long-distance work—things they enjoy doing. Then in November it's miles and miles of skiing. No interval work, just steady skiing. If a Norwegian's speed is off, he just enters more races. Each skier has a separate program. Except for a few big events each skier decides which races he wants to run.

"For them, training is training and racing is racing," Bob said, gesturing with the bread knife. "They know how to shift gears.

Racing

There are two kinds of racing: serious and fun. Often the two mix.

The fun events are the numerous "open" or "citizens" races sponsored by touring centers and ski clubs around New England. They are open to everybody and his grandmother, with results announced according to classes based on sex and age. Many races have mass starts, which in the case of the most famous annual competition of this kind, the Washington's Birthday Race in southern Vermont, meant 1000 people starting at once. (Abandoned by its original organizers for being too large, it has been given new life by the USEASA which will promote it in 1974 and thereafter.) Races are listed in the Appendix. They are mostly 10 to 15 kilometers. Some U.S. Team racers show off by entering them, which gives you the opportunity to say you raced against fellows like Mike Gallagher or Bob Gray. People have been known to pass wine bags back and forth in such events.

The NASTAR Alpine program now has its Nordic counterpart, generally to be found at downhill area touring centers. Anyone can enter. You race against a time set by a top competitor on a similar course. Awards are passed out, and there are NASTAR national championships. These are fun races, too.

The serious competition in New England is run under the aegis of the U.S. Eastern Amateur Ski Association, Littleton, N.H. (soon to relocate to Brattleboro, Vt.) A very extensive schedule exists. There is an Eastern Cross-Country Team whose members vie for berths on the U.S. Ski Team. Beneath the Eastern team are training squads and junior teams. Supplying these squads are club, high school and prep school teams. At the bottom is the Torger Tokle League, mostly sponsored by ski clubs. This is Nordic skiing's answer to the Buddy Werner League or Little League—for kids to age 13.

For those who don't want to race but who like to get medals anyhow, the U.S. Ski Association has a Distance Medal Events Log program. If you log 300 miles of touring on a special sheet—it's the honor system—and send it to the USSA with $7 for a USSA membership, you will receive a gold medal. Silver for 150 miles. Bronze for 75. Address: Distance Medal Events, USSA, 1726 Champa, Suite 300, Denver, Colo. 80202.

Start of the Paul Revere Cup Race. Bob, number three, shows perfect form right from the beginning while others scramble.

They don't mind hurting for a race. Our problem is we can't seem to separate in our minds training, which often seems a grind, from racing. We carry that grind thing over into racing. And the Norwegians try to make training something less of a grind, too. It's a *mental* thing. Look at Mike Gallagher. He's been measured. He's probably the best-trained athlete in the world. Our limitation is mental. For the Norwegians, their event is skiing. Races. You race for racing. You have to believe you can do it."

I had seen Gray race earlier in the year at the first Paul Revere Cup at Ft. Devens, Mass. He had come in 50 yards ahead of his nearest challengers, a pack of U.S. Ski Team members. Bob had won, on a 15-kilometer course, after waxing completely wrong— for granular snow when it turned out to be a blue klister day, extraordinarily icy. A newspaper account which stated he had double poled all the way, he said, was not too inaccurate. I told him I found it hard to believe that he didn't race for racing there.

He frowned, and his age showed in his eyes. "Look at Koch or Tim Caldwell," he responded. "They're used to going all out. They don't let them race 30 kilometers yet. Koch will be wiped out after a 10-kilometer race. You just have to go *all out*. And you have to ski well while doing it. It's almost a magical thing."

Mountain Touring: Katahdin

The tops of mountains are among the unfinished parts of the globe, whither it is a slight insult to the gods to climb and pry into their secrets, and try their effect on our humanity. Only daring and insolent men, perchance, go there. Simple races, as savages, do not climb mountains,—their tops are sacred and mysterious tracts never visited by them. Pomola is always angry with those who climb to the summit of Ktaadn.

HENRY DAVID THOREAU
The Maine Woods

IT WAS March and a poor snow year. The snow had already disappeared from much of Maine, but there was three or four feet at the Togue Pond entrance to Baxter State Park, where the plowed road stops. Here we started out late on a Friday afternoon up a snowmobiled road to Roaring Brook Campground, 10 miles north.

I had come to Baxter to test the limits of cross-country skiing in New England. Our destination was Katahdin, at 5267 feet the highest point in Maine and easily the most dramatic mountain in New England, rising alone in a blue and white massif from the green, flat north woods.

It may also be the most dangerous mountain in New England. Unlike Mount Washington, it is not readily accessible and on a given day there might be no one near it except you and your party. Rescue might be impossible and the weather can be murderous.

The trek in was a race between the skiers and the snowshoers, at least in some minds. Actually, it was not much of a contest: If anyone has any doubts which means of transport is fastest over varying and arduous terrain, this Katahdin trip is proof of the superiority of cross-country skis.

For example, Bob Cummings, a hardy fellow who's the environmental writer for the Portland papers, struck out on snowshoes from Togue Pond a good half hour before Andy Szelenyi and I did, but we passed Bob at the three-mile point and were in the vicinity of Roaring Brook an hour before he.

All we had to do was be sure of waxing right. It was blue wax going in. There were a couple of powdery inches over the crust, temperature in the low 20s, the sun occasionally piercing the overcast hiding the mountain. The hills were gentle; the elevation gain over the whole 10 miles was only a few hundred feet; there were even some fine downhill slopes. The spruce forest was quiet and after passing Bob we were breaking trail through the new powder. A fine run.

So fine, in fact—so fast a run—that we skied past the turnoff to Roaring Brook without noticing it. By the time Andy and I realized we had gone too far it was beginning to get dark. We hadn't left Togue Pond until well after three o'clock. So we scurried back to what looked like the campground road and hurried down it.

After a mile or so we stopped. Bob, when we had passed him, had told us we couldn't miss the camp—that it was "straight ahead." But we felt sure we had gone farther than 10 miles. It was getting darker and the temperature was dropping. Maybe we were on a trail we hadn't heard about. Bob had the map. We decided to go back to the turnoff and sliced quietly through the dusk.

Halfway back we met a couple of skiers in our party who had arrived at Togue Pond just as we left. They weren't sure if this was the Roaring Brook road either. They had followed our tracks. "It looks a lot different in the summer," one of them said.

But we concluded that we had better proceed down it anyway. By now it was pitch black, cold, and on a cloudy night the snow is not easily visible. Sometimes we couldn't see an incline or a dropoff ahead and we would experience alternating sensations of being driven into the snow feet first at moments when we weren't expecting a climb and our bodies hadn't made any adjustments for it, and of being lifted off the snow by our armpits when we suddenly found ourselves shooting downhill unexpectedly.

We went considerably farther down the road than Andy and I had the first time, and we stopped again. It still didn't look familiar to the fellow who had been here in the summer, and he thought we should have been at the campground long before now. We talked it over and decided to head back. We hoped we would reach the place we had turned off before Bob and the others had gone past.

By now frustration plus the rapid cooling of my previously sweaty body had tired me out, but we skied as fast as we could. My imagination spoke: Lost the first night near Katahdin! How would we live it down! We had packs, sleeping bags, stoves, food, and I I had a tube tent, so I didn't feel in danger—we knew the way out, so we weren't lost—but we weren't really prepared for a night in the woods.

It was with great relief that we met Bob trudging in, and he assured us we were on the correct route. He was slow on those snowshoes, but we were too fast. Too fast anyway to bother to get good directions and take the map, which is the moral of this episode. Although we were "in the vicinity" of Roaring Brook an hour or so before he was, as it turned out he got there about the same time as we.

We started down the road again, the third time for Andy and me. A little farther than where we had stopped the last time we arrived at the campground and located the bunkhouse with a flashlight. It was very simple: a small central room with a stove and a couple of tables and benches, and two rooms on either side filled with bunks and mattresses. Immediately we started building a fire, finding wood in a shed nearby.

As the wood was being lugged from the shed to the bunkhouse, we heard a loud whine and saw the lights of a snowmobile. A ranger from Togue Pond had come to check on us. "That's ranger wood," was the first thing he said. Andy stood looking at him. Visions of scrounging through the woods. The ranger smiled. "But

I guess you ain't going to get it anywhere else now."

He joined us in the quickly warmed cabin. I went down to the stream to get water, breaking through the crust up to my waist once off the skis. When I returned we had the essentials of a camp, fire and water, save one: firewater. So someone produced a flask of Southern Comfort, that drink of mountain men, and we all had a shot. A tradition to be honored.

We put some food on and greeted the others as they straggled in. Frank Roberts, the trip leader, soon showed up. Frank is a zoology professor at the University of Maine at Orono—quiet, trim, fortyish, salt-and-pepper hair, a mountaineer experienced in New England and the West. He is head of the wilderness committee of the Sierra Club's Maine chapter. This was a Sierra Club trip. Some of the people along were students at the University, and there were others—a boatbuilder and a laboratory worker from Mount Desert Island, for example.

Largely because of the good opinion Frank holds among the rangers, the requirements laid upon parties wishing to head up Katahdin were easily met. These, at the discretion of the park management, include doctors' certificates and specific plans for a rescue team. All that was required of us was to give Frank $3 a night to pay the rangers for use of the bunkhouse. I found out later, however, that he actually had arranged for a group of people to rescue us if necessary.

Saturday morning came early. Before dawn. Pity the people who got in at 2 a.m. But we were all up at once, groping, stretching, muttering. Breakfast for Andy, Bob and me was federal surplus powdered eggs donated by a low-income friend of Bob's, hot Tang, dried apricots, bread and cheese, dried salami diced up and mixed with the eggs, and coffee. All this was prepared and consumed instantly. Leaving camp when you want to go up Katahdin in winter must be done early and fast. The little butane stove I had packed came in handy; there was much demand for the lid of the wood stove.

Our immediate destination was Chimney Pond, 3.1 miles away

Skiers and snowshoers cross Chimney Pond heading into the South Basin. Directly ahead, cached in the clouds, is the summit.

and a couple of thousand feet up. Several left their skis at camp and donned the snowshoes they had brought. "You might not be able to make it on skis," Bob told us. He had been up the trail during the snow season, and it was steep.

But the climb turned out to be reprise of Friday, with Andy and I overtaking Bob and the other snowshoers soon after we left camp, even though they started before we did. We were both helped and hindered by the snowmobile tracks we followed. They had become crusty and the new powder had been blown off many sections. In some places there was blue ice. This made for a stiff climb. On the other hand, if we had had to wade through deep powder, I'm not sure we would have won the race with the snowshoers this time. But off the snowmobile trail the powder was only a few inches deep before the crust was found. The snowmobile tracks were made by the rangers' machines; other snowmobiles are limited to the so-called "perimeter" park roads where autos travel in the summer.

Again we had waxed right. Hard blue with a little red and purple mixed under foot. We poured it on going over the hills. The temperature was in the 20s and I stripped down to just a fish-net undershirt and a light turtleneck, but the sweat flowed into my eyes and I had to tie my bandanna into a headband to keep it out. We tried to ski straight up the pitches but at times were forced to herringbone and even to sidestep. My arm muscles did a lot of work, sometimes suspending me on my pole straps as the skis slid on the ice out from under me.

Near Basin Pond, about halfway, we got our first good look at Katahdin, not "Mount Katahdin" or "Katahdin Mountain." Katahdin, an Indian name, means "greatest mountain," and that is enough.

It appeared to be enough for us. Like an enormous grey altar it dominated the western sky, showing its stone in patches through the low clouds, great banks of snow leading up into the ravines. It looked ominous. We could not see the top. At times we could only see a low ridge and then a sweep of wind would reveal a whole mountainside, 2000-foot verticals and jagged silhouettes, where we had thought there was only sky. At once the entire Great Basin was before us, as suddenly it would disappear.

Thoreau tells of his pilgrimage to Katahdin:

> Occasionally, when the windy columns broke in to me, I caught sight of a dark, damp crag to the right or left; the mist driving ceaselessly between it and me. It reminded me of the creations of the old epic and dramatic poets, of Atlas, Vulcan, the Cyclops, and Prometheus. Such was Caucasus and the rock where Prometheus was bound. Aeschylus had no doubt visited such scenery as this. It was vast, Titanic, and such as man never inhabits. Some part of the beholder, even some vital part, seems to escape through the loose grating of his ribs as he ascends.

At Chimney Pond, a small lake at timberline covered with dune-like snowdrifts and set at the entrance to the deep South Basin, the skiers—four of us—waited for the rest of the party to catch up. We shared our food: cheese, liverwurst, raisins and lemonade. I had a special high-energy drink called Erg which everyone was interested in. It is supposed to get sugar into the blood stream as fast as it can be done short of injection. It was very refreshing after the climb.

Above us to our left as we faced west, Pamola, a craggy peak, emerged periodically from the clouds. To our right was the Cathedral, a steep mixture of ice and scree through which we planned to thread our way to Baxter Peak, the highest summit, which was always in the clouds. We watched the cloud show from the eastern shore of the lake not far from the unused ranger's cabin. This is a campground in the summer, and the only reason we wouldn't be camping there tonight was because another group had reserved the bunkhouse. A few years ago only several parties would try the mountain during the whole winter; now, several in a weekend were not uncommon.

Frank brought up the rear and as soon as he arrived we headed up, always up, towards the inside of the basin. We passed among stunted trees and over icy crust. It was very difficult with skis without steel edges. The slope became extremely steep.

Abruptly we reached the limits of cross-country skiing—the limits of going uphill, anyway: the slope gone to an impossible angle, the snow conditions equally impossible. We had gone as far as the snowshoers chose to go. Mountaineering skis, heavier and with steel edges, might have taken us a bit higher, and mountaineering skis with skins a little farther still, but not much. My Bonna 2000s, light touring skis, had taken me this far, and would get me down, and Katahdin is as demanding as any mountain in New England. What was needed now, and what would be needed at a similar point on Mount Washington, was crampons and an ice axe. Under a scraggly birch, at altitude 3600, we stacked our skis and snowshoes and put on those strange assemblies of steel spikes which are strapped to the feet.

Strange to me at least. Four of us had had no winter climbing

Picking their way through rock fields at timberline in the South Basin, the skiers soon reach the limits of their skis.

experience, and this was literally the first time Andy and I had stepped into crampons. We had told Frank we intended to go only as far as our experience warranted and for him not to feel badly if he had to tell us to turn back. He had said that we probably could hike quite a ways up with little skill, but it was clear that he was disconcerted at how little our little skill amounted to. For me it included not knowing how to get my crampons on.

At this point, after some discussion, Frank prevailed upon the group to abandon the Cathedral and with it hopes of reaching Baxter Peak. It was too cloudy and windy, he said. The group might lose the trail and there would be nothing to see anyway if the summit were achieved.

We decided to head up the Chimney, a steep but snow-filled chute which is a technical rock-climbing route in the summer. The route went directly up the south side of the basin to the Knife

Edge, the main southern ridge of the mountain, and from there it was a short climb to the summit of Pamola, named for an Indian god that inhabits Katahdin. Pamola, which was often free of clouds, was to be the destination, only a few hundred feet lower than Baxter.

We began the ascent with Frank instructing the neophytes in elementary ice-axe technique: how to hold it across the body and how to self-arrest by digging the point in to stop a fall by bringing your weight down on the axe. We were taught how to step with the crampons. Somebody lent me overboots, which look like booted gaiters that come to the knees and Bob gave me his extra pair of heavy-weather mittens. As we filed carefully up the slope, using the axes as canes at first, I felt as if I must certainly be playing a part in a movie about the conquest of some Himalayan giant.

The view was Himalayan. Surprisingly soon we were far above the tiny dot that represented our cache of equipment. We looked down upon Chimney Pond and far beyond to Katahdin Lake at the edge of the park.

Soon we were into the chute. Rock walls straight up on either side. Crusty snow alternating with deep powder. One slow step at a time we moved up along the side of the chimney, the foot brought to the level of the knee with each step. Patricia Albert, an Orono student, led much of the way; then Frank took over. The boat-builder from Mount Desert Island was putting little route marker flags in the snow. Above us, nearly vertically above us, the top of the chute seemed tantalizingly near, white puffs blowing fast across the blue sky framed by the rock and snow. "We can go a little further before we have to rope up," Frank said when we stopped to rest.

Then, we reached a sheer bed of bluish ice. Everyone prepared to rope up. Everyone but the inexperienced. "I wouldn't advise you to go any further," Frank said. Reluctantly, we took the advice.

We watched and photographed as the band chipped away at the ice for footholds and handholds and inched up, three on a rope. Cold blasts every now and then blew down the chute, but the climbing party was happy. The weather was much better than on previous trips to Katahdin, and it would be an easy climb.

We four who remained were not really unhappy. We decided to try a way of getting down that we had heard the mountaineers talking about—glissading, French for sliding. On your bottom.

Zoom! Off like mini-avalanches we were, steadying ourselves with our ice axes, slowing ourselves by digging our feet into the snow. Around the curves of the chute and into the open of the basin in seconds. Presto, the sun! A thrill to be recommended highly.

For Andy and me, the ski back to Roaring Brook was just as exciting. We flew. The section from Chimney to Basin Pond was so steep and the trail so narrow and curving that many times we would have to sit on our skis and drag our hands to slow down. There is nothing quite like ripping around a curve, banking on

With ice axes and crampons, the group climbs up into the Chimney. The last man places route markers in the snow.

your left haunch, to meet a series of bumps which you have to take in one leap, with only the tails of your skis on the snow, besides your rear end. The limits of cross-country skiing, downhill version—at least without the heels bound down and without steel edges. Mountaineering skis and bindings would have helped here.

From Basin to Roaring Brook it was slightly less steep; we could stand up more often, knees flexed, weight on the heels, skis flat on the snow except when snowplowing into the powder along the side of the trail or when making quick step turns. Total concentration on the trail was necessary, yet I couldn't help enjoying the spruce, birch, fir and pine, a chipmunk caught out of the corner of the eye, the rushing stream, the glint of the sun through bare branches. The joy of cross-country skiing, downhill version.

Late afternoon shadows were spreading over the snow when we skied into camp. We quickly had the fire blazing, filled up the canteens and pots with water from the stream, and when Bob arrived he started making a big pot of meat (several kinds) and vegetable stew. Everything from the supermarket but nothing in cans. We found we all disdained freeze-dried backpacking food as too expensive.

The climbers appeared, exhausted, just at dark—surprisingly quick, I thought, but they had of course glissaded too. They had climbed Pamola easily, and Frank graciously said that we could have probably made it. They were as impressed with our ski down from Chimney Pond as we were with their ascent.

The evening was devoted to stories around the stove, many about the treacherous, unbelievably harsh weather that frequents Katahdin in the winter, but which we fortunately missed. It was late in the season, although March can be a bad month. We sipped bourbon from regulation Sierra Club cups and retired early.

We were again up early. The skiers' question of the morning was what to wax. It was spitting snow but the temperature was rapidly rising. Since we would be going downhill, I decided to wax fast and slapped on a little more blue.

Sure enough, it was fast. It was all right for a while, until it started raining and the trail glazed over. Bob had begun a good three-quarters of an hour before we did this time, but we soon passed him. I was travelling at about 30 miles per hour, completely out of control. Wham! My personal cyclone of skis and arms. Bob trudged by smiling. I was off again, smiling myself as I wooshed by. Bam! Nose first into the crust. Again Bob plodded by. That wonderful spirit of trail competition.

This wasn't quite a classic tortoise and hare story. Andy and I beat him by half an hour. It was a hair-rising ride into Togue Pond, though, and we raised a few bruises as well.

All in all, Pamola smiled on us this time. But then we didn't go to the summit.

Big Mountains

To tackle Katahdin, you should be a serious skier in good condition. The whole of Baxter State Park, a land designated "forever wild," provides many opportunities for serious skiing—many less difficult than Katahdin.

There are a number of bunkhouses and shelters in the park available to the public in the winter. Permission and reservations are required from the Baxter Park Authority in Millinocket. Bob Cummings once traversed the length of the 200,000-acre preserve with a group of skiers and snowshoers. They stayed at these cabins.

Be careful. Be a good scout: Be prepared. Katahdin has killed the careless and unprepared. In December, January and February, the temperature often drops to 30 below zero. For this reason, late-season skiing—March and April—presents fewer dangers.

Similar dangers await the unprepared on the upper reaches of Mount Washington and a few of the other Presidentials. See the section on Appalachian Mountain Club trails in New Hampshire for more on this subject.

Touring & the Ecology

A CALL TO ARMS

I HAVE an issue of a skiing magazine in which there is a piece entitled "I Love Touring, But . . ." Here are a few quotes from it: "One of the major myths affecting cross-country: You can jump on your skis anytime there are a few inches of snow on the ground and go galloping across any old bit of countryside . . . This go-anywhere myth is linked with a couple of hypes—namely, that cross-country will take you back to nature and that it's the ultimate do-it-yourself sport . . . Let's stop thinking of ourselves as hikers and backpackers on skis . . . We'll have to drop another myth, that touring is skiing on the cheap."

The article is wrong on every point. This is a classic example of the kind of thinking many old-time tourers fear will spoil the sport. This kind of thinking usually has as its source the commercial motive, and its manifestations are expensive equipment and clothes, and special places to stay and tour—also expensive. These remarks cannot do otherwise than please the magazine's advertisers—the manufacturers of equipment and clothing, the proprietors of resorts and inns.

How can touring be spoiled? It's such an essentially *simple* sport. Let those who want to pay high prices and spend their time in Alpine environments do it. But there's no way they can force you to dance to their numbers, you say.

Well, the old-timer responds, just look how those simple skis you buy have gone up in price through the years. And, he says, if you care about whether other people are being bilked, and whether they're having the pleasure they should, you have to care about such a thing as the commercialization of ski touring.

This is quite a controversy in the world of touring, a controversy most people touring for the first time probably aren't aware of. Many people, however, are afraid that touring will go the way of Alpine skiing.

Well, I don't think it will. I believe in that essential physical simplicity of the sport and the restrictions this places upon exploitation. Touring isn't dependent on motors. It is based on the values of self-reliance and solitude. And I'm not convinced commercialization will bring only evils. Some of the "commercial" inns I've been

to, with their conviviality and the opportunity they present of meeting people who share interests, rank as some of the finer experiences I've had in my touring seasons. Some of the prepared tracks I've skied on rank as some of the best places I've skied. I, too, am fascinated by the products of technology and like to profit from them. Although I think taking off on one's own down some tree-walled woods road is the ultimate experience in the sport, I realize that many people are not ready for this. I have seen people so utterly ill-at-ease in the outdoors and on skis that I couldn't help but think that they needed a good paid lesson. Also, to some degree I try to get along with the inevitable. Most of the touring in Scandinavia is done on prepared trails, and I'm under no illusion that our situation a few years from now is going to be any better. It should be as good.

But I still am worried. It's that advertising. That advertising that might scare people away from the sport. When touring fashions appear in *Vogue,* ski prices double, and trail fees abound, you begin to wonder if the average Joe or Jane will even look at the sport that seemed tailor-made for them.

You see, if touring develops in the proper manner—if the word that gets out about it is undistorted—it has the potential of a true mass sport, as it is in Norway, Sweden and Finland.

It would be a much more beneficial mass sport than that of opening pop-top beer cans as we watch football on TV. Unlike many other nations, we seem to specialize in sports that nobody has

---

Opening Your Eyes

Ski touring's pleasure can be heightened immeasureably if you take a keen interest in what's going on around you in the winter woods. Some people shut off their senses in the winter. True hibernators, they. Instead, take advantage of your new-found mobility and discover the delights of wintertime—each delight to be separately and clearly perceived, unlike summer's overwhelming lushness.

Look for birds. Good places would be in the Audubon sanctuaries, or in the numerous National Wildlife Refuges, all open to tourers. Write for a descriptive brochure, "National Wildlife Refuges in the Northeast," Bureau of Sport Fisheries and Wildlife, U.S. Department of the Interior, Washington, D.C. Numerous bird species winter in New England: mallard, partridge, screech and horned owl, downy woodpecker, goldfinch, nuthatch, junco, and of course the common blue jay, crow, chickadee, starling. There are many others. Get a field guide to help you and keep a list.

Watch for mammals. They are harder to see in the snow time, but their tracks are abundant: deer, gray and red squirrels, rabbits and hares, deer mice, shrews, foxes, and—in the real wilds—coyotes, moose and bear. Bears, raccoons, chipmunks and skunks venture from their sleep during mild weather. Many animal guides have drawings of tracks.

Many tree and shrub guides have pages of information on identification by winter silhouettes and twig forms. The *Winter Tree Finder,* put out by the Nature Study Guide, Box 972, Berkeley, Calif. 94701,

much chance of participating in past the age of 20. Touring is something everybody can do. Cross-country is the perfect secondary school sport: inexpensive; individualistic, yet it can be a team sport; for everybody, yet it can be intensely competitive; and it appeals to contemporary kids who are interested in getting into the outdoors.

If touring became a mass sport, it would strengthen the hand of all those interested in preserving the winter wilderness and just plain woods from becoming the exclusive domain of snowmobilers and, in the mountains, downhill ski area developers.

Touring is an undamaging sport to the environment. Unlike downhill skiing, it doesn't concentrate people into, for the environ-

---

is devoted to winter identification.

The cold, clear nights of winter provide an unexcelled opportunity for star gazing. Ski a little way from your town's lights and scan other worlds and galaxies with a pair of field glasses.

During the day, become an amateur meteorologist. Do you know what cirrus clouds are? What they may mean? When the wind backs into the south, what is happening? Knowing how to read the skies, especially with the aid of a pack thermometer and pocket barometer, may help you conduct your outings better. For example, you will know when to hurry home.

Reading the landscape is easier in the winter when the land is stripped of its covering foliage. Do you know the features of our glacial geography? Do you know when you're skiing on a drumlin or an esker? You've never explored a glacial cirque? Then go to Tuckerman's Ravine. The huge boulders around you—what are they composed of and where did they come from? *A Guide to New England's Landscape* by Neil Jorgensen (Barre, $3.95) contains many answers, and it is also a guide to the botany of our region.

Finally, what about exploring our folkways? End a full day of touring by skiing to a church supper in a Yankee village. Did you know that the tiny, out-of-the-way town of Richmond, Maine, has an inexpensive, authentic Russian restaurant? The town is a Russian colony complete with an Orthodox church.

Open eyes mean you're not sleeping through life.

ment and their own spirit, a destructive force which can explode its effects over wide areas. Millions tour in Scandinavia, and the countryside is preserved. Millions could tour in the United States and there still would be plenty of places to get away from others.

Unless something is done soon, downhill ski resorts are going to gobble up the best of our mountains in much the same way that second-home developments are eating away at shoreline and lakefront. Anybody who has ever visited ski areas during the summer knows that those scarred mountains are pretty much destroyed for hiking or camping. The wilderness is cracked apart right up to the drilling on the highest summits to install pylons for the gondolas. Ski areas ignore the ecology, but their pressure on the remaining wild land is enormous. I have an article clipped from the Sunday New York Times travel section in which a moaning and groaning is heard because Vermont has seen fit to question, from the environmental point of view, the future development of the ski industry. Already, the article says, because of this obstructionism some ski areas are instituting reserved lift ticket policies. What are the increasing numbers of downhill skiers to do if they can't have all the mountains? A Vermont official suggests cross-country skiing. His suggestion is scornfully compared to Marie Antoinette's "Let them eat cake."

Even for the more remote mountains the dangers are imminent. Already, Bigelow Mountain, Maine's "second mountain," and one of our most magnificant, is being eyed covetously for a huge Alpine resort.

But imagine a cross-country ski and snowshoe "development" for Bigelow: a single lodge in a remote valley serviced by snow-vehicle shuttles; huts could be built with a network of trails. Hundreds, even thousands, could use the area and its ecological character would be preserved.

I realize a handful of readers will object to even this development for our remaining mountains, but I think the choice will be between something like this and the motorized steel-edged juggernaut which is rapidly tearing into the forests.

As a broad alternative, why not maintain networks of huts and trails for hundreds of miles through many of our mountains and wild areas for the use of ski tourers, snowshoers, and hikers? The Appalachian Mountain Club, because of the interest in touring, is opening its huts in the winter. Huts like these are widespread in Scandinavian and Alpine countries. They could be shelters or hostels —cheap, simple, nonprofit inns.

There would be a way to do this. And a way to assure that ski touring isn't coopted, "spoiled." Touring skiers could organize. Organized, they could provide free whatever lessons are needed, map and maintain trails, buy equipment wholesale, propagandise, lobby. They could join with other outdoors people—hikers, mountaineers, snowshoers, canoeists, fishermen, hunters. They could organize from scratch or they could try to revive the community ski clubs of New England, many of which became moribund as skiing became less and less a sport for everybody and more and more for the affluent.

I realize I'm bucking the Great American Traditions of spending lots of money for recreation and of moving about only with the aid of motors. But as Huck Finn says: "All right, then, I'll go to hell." Pick up the banner of ecology along with your cross-country skis.

It's Beautiful
& It's Morally Straight

I WOULD like to convince everybody to take up ski touring. Not just for the good it does the body, but for what it does to the spirit. I hear myself sounding like the football coach of my high school years, so let me adopt a different voice. I think of the poet Sylvia Plath, a New Englander, and a phrase of hers I'll never forget: "stewing in my own sour air." Unpleasant thought. But that's what I think about so many people who never *release* themselves in any way. They're stewing in their own juices.

Release is what athletics is all about, and it's what art is all about. Athletics is art. They both provide the release of, the liberation of, in various mixes, the mind and the body. As it has been asked: What essential difference is there between a dancer flying across a stage and a quarterback snaking gracefully down a field?

Those we call true artists—that is, those who excell, be it in football or ski racing or ballet or painting—are those who most release their imagination, as well as their bodies and intellect.

It is possible to release the imagination by being a spectator—by watching football on TV or going to a concert or reading a good book. But I would argue that direct participation is more healthful than vicarious experience. It provides more of an opportunity for release, to escape from stewing. What we need is a nation of skiers, dancers and poets.

Participation, action, art, athletics are all needed more than ever in a society where technology and sheer numbers have made it so simple to sit and stew—watching TV, being carried about by machines. When we move we are forced into narrow, crowded physical and mental corridors. Herd 'em up, move 'em out.

Stewing in one's own juices may mean you can't touch or be touched by others. You are encapsulated. You cry for release. But technological society makes release more difficult than ever before.

Yet it can be effected.

Maybe ski touring won't answer all your problems, give you complete release, give you liberation of the self by an affirmation of the self and its powers of body, mind and imagination, but I'll guarantee you it will answer some problems. And it's a good way to ease into creative modes of being.

SELF-RELIANCE AND SOLITUDE

These have been referred to as the special values of touring, but they are the rewards of any individual activity in the outdoors.

They are to some degree the special values of New Englanders, and, as for self-reliance, Ralph Waldo Emerson has pretty much said it all in his famous essay.

> The civilized man has built a coach, but has lost the use of his feet. He is supported on crutches, but lacks so much support of muscles. He has a fine Geneva watch, but he fails of the skill to tell the hour by the sun. A Greenwich nautical almanac he has, and so being sure of the information when he wants it, the man in the street does not know a star in the sky. The solstice he does not observe; the equinox he knows as little; and the whole bright calendar of the year is without a dial in his mind.

Suffice it to say that probably never before have these values been more neglected than today with our mass society and techno-logical dependence.

The needs for the solace of solitude and reliance upon the self are correspondingly greater than ever before. Getting out by your-self on two skis through the quiet beauty of the winter woods for a few hours can be a balm to the most city-troubled mind. There is within us all the need for that wonderfully childish activity—to go "exploring."

This does not mean you have to be entirely alone. There is in a tour with a few friends or even strangers an aura of solitude and self-respect around each individual which can serve as the basis for authentic relationships, real friendships or at least friendliness—situations impossible when pursuing an activity of the herd, in which little can be authentic since the gesture has taken the place of the action; that is, every action is predetermined by the advertising cliche that encompasses it, or status-seeking, one-up-manship and other forms of snobbery dominate all feelings.

I do not hesitate to recommend getting out in the woods alone, and I realize that I am now uttering heresy. It's ridiculous to say to mature people who have taken some trouble to prepare themselves in the ways of the wilds that they can't receive what nature has to offer when confronted alone, or with one friend. They'll do it anyway; I don't know a single experienced outdoorsman or skier who doesn't go into the woods alone occasionally. Risk exacts its measure, however—sometimes you lose. But I'd rather lose in the woods than anywhere else.

"Trust thyself: every heart vibrates to that iron string," said Emerson.

THE LAST TOUR

It was a quiet night. I went outside to check the temperature and to look at the stars. Twenty-two degrees. Cassiopeia blinked above a fir tree.

I tasted the silence. Andy and I were perhaps 10 miles from anyone else, from human noise. The stream rushed by the cabin, but its sound seemed at one with the stillness. It was peaceful standing there in the snow beneath the silver-black starry sky, the moon a shimmering brightness on the edge of a ridge. Yet, I must confess that—once a little away from the cabin and with no flashlight—the darkness made me the slightest bit uneasy. I am used to the woods and have no distaste for darkness—often I welcome it. But standing there it was suddenly clear to me how some people could be frightened by the wilderness.

The next day we skied down to the valley floor. The crusty snow dazzled us. It glinted like armor, encasing everything except the few spruce and fir. But the fresh powder hadn't been blown off the western slope, where there were more trees, and we effortlessly sliced down to the stream. We found a large stump, a perfect spot for lunch.

The sun was warm, the sky cloudless. We were very much alone in that remote valley, and it occurred to me, as I munched my salami and cheese, that the size of the cliffs on either side and the sky could have been intimidating, could have shrunk me. Instead I seemed to expand. A loss of ego, but I felt my personal importance in this scene. It was, rather, an openness. I felt as open as the sky. There, then, as at few other times in my life, I felt, yes, at one with everything around me. With just the right touch of self-consciousness. It felt good to be personally part of it all. Reassurance. A good reason to go into the mountains.

The rest of the afternoon the going got rougher. Once we had to inch along the side of a ravine, stamping out secure tracks in the crumbly snow. Below was a torrent, which we were forced to cross on a snow bridge. We stopped on the rim of a ridge as the weak sun turned the rocks golden around us. We skimmed swiftly back down through the valley's shadow, the snow now glazed with ice. The wind stung our faces.

Trail Maps & Guides

Ski Touring Guide, Ski Touring Council, c/o Rudolph Mattesich, West Hill Road, Troy, Vt. 05868. $1.75. No maps, good descriptions and directions. New England and New York trails, a few elsewhere in the East. Some general touring information.

Ski Touring Guide to New England, Eastern Mountain Sports, 1041 Commonwealth Ave., Boston, Mass. 02215. Many maps, but almost unreadable. Ample descriptions and directions. Good on Massachusetts and New Hampshire. Only a trail guide.

White Mountains Ski Touring Club trail description brochure, White Mountains Region Association, Lancaster, N.H. 03584. Brief descriptions.

White Mountain Guide, Maine Mountain Guide, Massachusetts and Rhode Island Trail Guide, Appalachian Mountain Club, 5 Joy St., Boston, Mass. 02108. Not touring guides, but many hiking trails are fine for touring.

The following books may also be purchased from the A.M.C. (send for publications pamphlet and price list):

Guide to the Appalachian Trail in New Hampshire and Vermont, Guide to the Appalachian Trail in Maine, Guide to the Appalachian Trail in Massachusetts and Connecticut, Metacomet-Monadnock Trail Guide, Monadnock Guide, Long Trail Guide, Connecticut Walk Book, Dartmouth Outing Club Trail Guide.

U.S. Geological Survey maps can be purchased in many sporting goods stores. Or order directly. Send for a free Topographic Map Index Circular of the state you are interested in, and for the booklet, Topographic Maps. Address: U.S. Geological Survey, 1200 South East St., Arlington, Va. 22202.

National forests, Acadia National Park, state parks, forests and reservations, private forests, and Audubon sanctuaries have maps. Many references, with addresses, are made to these in the text. And most touring centers have trail maps, many with accompanying trail descriptions.

Annual Open Races

MAINE

Rangeley Ramble, Rangeley. Sponsored by the Nordic Ski Club of Rangeley. January. Since 1972. Mass start. 10 kilometers. 80 participants in 1973. Open to all. Write to David Lanzo, Rangeley.

Sunday River Langlauf, Bethel. Sponsored by the Sunday River Ski Club. 2nd Sunday in March. Since 1973. Mass start. 7 and 14 kilometers. Open to all. Race begins and ends at Sunday River Inn. Free refreshments, $1 lunch. Trophies and ribbons. Write to Sunday River Inn, Bethel 04217.

NEW HAMPSHIRE

Waterville Valley Cross-Country Ski Touring Derby, Waterville Valley. February. Since 1973. Mass start. 10 kilometers. 120 in first race. Open to all. Race begins at ski touring center. Free refreshments. Band serenades. Many medals. Write to Don Johnsen, Ski Touring Director, Waterville Valley.

VERMONT

Madonna Vasa. Madonna Ski Area, Jeffersonville. 1st Sunday in March. Coincides with Swedish Vasaloppet. Since 1965. Skiers take off at 30-second intervals. Rugged 20-kilometer course begins at Madonna Ski Area. Open to all racers, ski tourers not admitted. Write to William Bull, 17 East Terrace, South Burlington.

Stowe Derby, Stowe. March. Since 1965. Two courses, longest is 10.6 miles. Open to all. Prizes and dances in evening. Write to George S. Prouty Jr., Stowe 05672.

Blueberry Hill Annual Cross-Country Race and Pig Roast, Brandon. March. Since 1970. 7 miles. 250 in last race. Tour or race on course and then eat barbecued pig. Edible prizes. Open to all. Write Blueberry Hill Farm, Brandon 05733.

Washington's Birthday Ski Touring Race, Brattleboro. Abandoned by the original organizers as being too large and unwieldy. Revived as we go to press by the United States Eastern Amateur Ski Association. Start and finish in Brattleboro. Contact the USEASA, 22 High St., Brattleboro, Vermont 05301.

MASSACHUSETTS

Paul Revere Cup, Ft. Devens. Sponsored by American Nordic Skiing Association. February. Since 1973. 15 kilometers. 300 in first race. Open to all. Mass start. Certificates awarded. Write to American Nordic Skiing Association, Concord 01742

CONNECTICUT

Great Race, West Simsbury. Sponsored by Ski Touring Association. February. Since 1973. 5 kilometers. Open to all. Mass start. Refreshments. Write to Great World Inc., 250 Farms Village Rd., West Simsbury 06092.